CANADA'S **BEST**
SLOW COOKER
RECIPES

To John

Everything in here
is for Gary! I hope
you enjoy it.
all the best!
Donna-Marie Pye.

CANADA'S **BEST**
SLOW COOKER
RECIPES

Robert
ROSE

Canada's Best Slow Cooker Recipes

For complete cataloguing information, see page 6.

DESIGN, EDITORIAL AND PRODUCTION:	MATTHEWS COMMUNICATIONS DESIGN INC.
PHOTOGRAPHY:	MARK T. SHAPIRO
ART DIRECTION, FOOD PHOTOGRAPHY:	SHARON MATTHEWS
FOOD STYLIST:	KATE BUSH
PROP STYLIST:	CHARLENE ERRICSON
MANAGING EDITOR:	PETER MATTHEWS
INDEX:	BARBARA SCHON
COLOR SCANS & FILM:	POINTONE GRAPHICS

Cover image: ZESTY ORANGE BEEF STEW (PAGE 116)

We acknowledge the financial support of the Government of Canada through the Book Publishing Industry Development Program (BPIDP) for our publishing activities.
Canadä

Published by: Robert Rose Inc. • 120 Eglinton Ave. E., Suite 1000
Toronto, Ontario, Canada M4P 1E2   Tel: (416) 322-6552   Fax: (416) 322-6936

Printed in Canada
34567 BP 03 02 01 00

Table of Contents

Canadian Cataloguing in Publication Data

Pye, Donna-Marie
   Canada's best slow cooker recipes

Includes index.
ISBN 0-7788-0024-5

1. Electric cookery, Slow. 2. Casserole cookery. I. Title.

TX827.P933 2000   641.5'884   C00-931303-6

To my mom

Evelyn Pye

who taught me to love good food,

and my family,

Lawrence, Darcy and Jack

— the reason I *keep* cooking and enjoying good food.

Acknowledgements

Writing a cookbook didn't seem like such a huge task when the idea was first presented to me. But the reality has proven to be quite different. After many hours of testing, tasting and revising, I managed to accomplish the job – but wouldn't have, were it not for the support of my family, friends and colleagues to whom I owe so many thanks for making this book a reality.

To my neighbor, assistant, expert taste-tester and, most important, invaluable friend, Joanne Burton, who spent countless hours typing and editing this manuscript because she thought this would be an enjoyable project to tackle after finding herself with a little more time on her hands, once her youngest child headed off to school full-time.

My publisher, Bob Dees, for his dedication and encouragement, and to the whole team at Robert Rose for making my recipes better and better, and for a beautiful book.

Heartfelt thanks go to my Tuesday-morning quilt group, whose members – Kathy Shortt, Karen Scian, Susan McDowell and Martha D'Agostino – lovingly sampled every dish I toted along and gave up an entire day of quilting to help edit the book.

My mother and father, Evelyn and Roger Pye, for their constant support despite giving up important hours on the golf course to trek through supermarkets in the southern U.S., checking out product sizes, labels and names. And to my mother-in-law and father-in-law, Mary and Chris Greaves, for their encouraging words and editorial advice.

My sisters, Sandy and Glenda, who willingly subjected their families to the recipes I tested, and passed along great suggestions.

My colleague, Wendy Heibert, for her fine-tuning skills and encouraging words.

The many neighbors and friends who welcomed me into their kitchens with my recipes, lent me their slow cookers and shared their recipes and cooking know-how (or know-not-how) about slow cooking. Jenna Jutzi and Meghan Pierce, who spent many after-school hours, caring for my children, Darcy and Jack, giving me that all-important extra hour of writing or testing time when I most needed it.

To the many organizations and companies who gave products, information and permission to adapt their recipes for this book, including *Canadian Living* Magazine, the Delft Blue Veal Company, the Ontario Turkey Producers' Marketing Board, the Ontario Pork and the Beef Information Center.

And finally, to my husband Lawrence for his love and support, but mainly for his patience.

Introduction

For many years, my job required a lengthy commute – about 90 minutes each way, every day. That meant leaving early in the morning and coming home to face the daily dilemma of what to have for dinner. While the family consisted of just my husband and me, we muddled along. But once we had children, I decided to enlist the help of a kitchen assistant – my slow cooker.

At least once a week, I would prepare all the ingredients for my favorite soup, stew or pot roast in my slow cooker insert and leave the assembled dish in the refrigerator overnight. The next morning, I would slip the insert into the slow cooker and the food would simmer away all day while I was at work. My family certainly enjoyed coming home and eating a hot dinner right away, rather than having to wait until 8:00 at night. As a bonus, there were always enough leftovers for a meal later in the week.

While no longer commuting, I am now a freelance home economist, busy wife and mother raising a 7-year-old daughter and 4-year-old son. A full schedule of work commitments, volunteer activities and the children's soccer practice, swimming, dance and music lessons, doesn't leave much time to prepare a hot meal at the end of the day. It still makes sense to turn on the slow cooker and have dinner ready and waiting when we get home.

In writing this book, my goal was to keep it family-friendly and to cook with ingredients and use recipes that would appeal to a busy family like mine. Some require long slow cooking and others may not take quite as long, but my family and friends have been quite surprised at how many different dishes can be prepared in the slow cooker. This book contains everything from warm starters such as HOT CRAB, ARTICHOKE AND JALAPEÑO SPREAD and APPLE CINNAMON SIPPERS to dinnertime classics such as HOMESTYLE POT ROAST, COUNTRY-STYLE HONEY GARLIC RIBS, NEW ENGLAND-STYLE CLAM CHOWDER and COQ AU VIN. Meatloaf is so juicy and moist that I am convinced that I will never cook it any other way. The slow cooker even makes an impressive array of desserts such as STEAMED CRANBERRY PUDDING WITH GRAND MARNIER SAUCE and UPSIDE-DOWN FUDGE BROWNIE PUDDING, as well as delicious fruit cobblers and an outstanding AUNT BEATTY'S BETTY.

So try the recipes in this book – and get ready to discover all the amazing food you can make with your slow cooker!

– Donna-Marie Pye

All about slow cooking

The first slow cookers, designed primarily as a device for cooking baked beans, were introduced over 25 years ago as The Rival Company's Crock-Pot® Stoneware Slow Cooker. Since then, millions of people across North America have discovered the amazing versatility of this appliance. And slow cookers continue to be one of today's most popular household appliances.

Why slow cook?

Slow cookers are ideally suited to meeting the needs of today's busy families. Their advantages include:

Convenience. Because the appliance cooks with such low heat, food won't scorch so it doesn't require tending. Once you add the ingredients to the slow cooker and turn it on, you can forget about it and devote your time to other activities. At the end of the day, you and your family can still enjoy a hot, nutritious, home-cooked meal with minimal effort. Most recipes can be assembled the night before, refrigerated in the stoneware bowl and cooked the following day. The slow cooker is especially handy when entertaining or cooking for a large crowd, since it frees you from the kitchen and allows you to spend time with your guests. And because you can use your slow cooker as a serving bowl, that's one less thing to clean up afterwards.

Economy. Basically the slow cooker works by simmering food at a constant, low temperature which enhances the flavor and texture of some ingredients. Slow cooking tenderizes less expensive cuts of meat such as beef brisket, stewing beef and pork, pork shoulder roasts and chops. The lengthy cooking time tenderizes these tougher cuts

of meat and allows the flavors to blend, resulting in the tastiest soups, stews, chilies and pot roasts.

Dried beans, peas and lentils are an economical alternative to canned, and can be cooked very easily in the slow cooker. Once cooked, simply add them to soups and chilies for a delicious one-pot meal.

Practicality. Because it cooks primarily with moisture, there is virtually no sticking with the slow cooker. (For some dishes – such as desserts, puddings and custards – I recommend that you lightly grease the bowl first, to make cleaning even easier.) The appliance also runs on very little electricity. And it's perfect for warm weather months, when using a conventional oven would make the kitchen uncomfortably warm. The slow cooker also frees up valuable oven space when entertaining or cooking for a crowd. It is ideal for cooking holiday side dishes and, as noted earlier, you can even serve from it.

Types of slow cookers

Today's slow-cooking appliances fall into two basic categories:

Multi-cookers. These have an adjustable thermostat, so they can be used for a variety of cooking methods that include slow cooking, deep-frying and steaming. In most multi-cookers the heating coil is located in the base of the housing unit so the heat comes from the bottom. Some models of this type of cooker come with a crockery insert, which can help to distribute the heat more evenly. However, food prepared in a multi-cooker should still be watched carefully and stirred two or three times during the cooking time to prevent sticking. The advantage to this type of unit is that you can easily speed up the cooking time simply by adjusting the thermostat to a higher setting.

Slow cookers. Essentially a contemporary version of The Rival Company's Crock-Pot® Stoneware Slow Cooker, this type of cooker usually features a metal casing with electric heating coils surrounding a heavy stoneware or ceramic bowl. The stoneware may or may not be removable, but the removable type is preferable for ease of cleaning. (Some manufacturers have introduced slow cookers with a nonstick stoneware surface that makes cleaning even easier.) The stoneware acts as an excellent insulator and keeps the cooking temperature even and low. As the food begins to heat up, a seal is formed between the stoneware and the covering lid. This keeps the liquid inside from evaporating and virtually eliminates the risk of sticking and scorching. As a result, the food doesn't require constant attention and can be left unattended for several hours.

How big a slow cooker do you need?

Slow cookers come in round or oval shapes and range in capacity from 2 1/2 to 6 quarts. (Multicookers are generally oval-shaped and can be used for everyday cooking and roasting.) The 2 1/2- and 3 1/2-quart sizes are usually deep and narrow; 4- and 5-quart size are wider and rounder. All are perfect for soups, stews, pot roasts, casseroles and everyday cooking. The large 6-quart size is best for big-batch cooking, for steamed puddings or for recipes that call for large pieces of meat such as corned beef or brisket. In this size of slow-cooker, for a roast larger than that called for in a recipe,

you will need to increase the cooking time (on **Low**) by 1 1/2 hours per additional pound (500 g) to ensure it is tender.

Slow cookers also come in a 1-quart size. Although too small for everyday cooking, it is great for warm dips and appetizers, and perfect for entertaining. Most of the recipes in this book were tested in the 3 1/2- and 4-quart size of slow cooker. But unless otherwise specified, most can be made in any size of slow cooker, except the 1-quart size. For the dessert lover, the 4- and 5-quart size are best, because they hold a 6-cup bowl or pudding mold.

When you shouldn't use a slow cooker

Although it's great for many foods, the slow cooker doesn't cook everything well. The secret, as with all appliances, is to use it for what it does best. Foods that don't benefit from slow cooking include:

• Large, tender cuts of meat such as leg of lamb or prime rib roasts. These are best roasted in a conventional oven.

• Pasta becomes very glutinous when added dry to the slow cooker. It is best to parboil pasta to the tender-but-firm stage, drain, then add to your slow cooker recipe.

• Fish does not hold up well in the slow cooker. Because it is so tender, it will fall apart, leaving you with nothing but flaked fish. You can still make fish recipes, however, but the fish should only be added during the last 20 minutes of cooking time. There are a few exceptions, such as KID'S FAVORITE TUNA NOODLE CASSEROLE, SIMPLE SALMON PIE WITH CREAMY DILL SAUCE and EASY JAMBALAYA.

While it uses only a gentle heat, the slow cooker can still overcook food. It is important to try to adhere to the recommended cooking times in the recipes.

Care and cleaning of your slow cooker

After cooking and before cleaning, allow the lid and the stoneware bowl to cool. To avoid any extreme temperature changes, do not place hot lid or stoneware into cold water or onto a cold, wet surface. The stoneware can safely be washed in hot soapy water or in the dishwasher. In the latter case, I recommend giving the bowl a short soak in hot water first, particularly if you have any stubborn cooked-on food. New stoneware with nonstick coatings have made this less of a problem.

Never use harsh, abrasive cleansers or scouring pads, since this can scratch the stoneware. The base only needs a wipe with a damp cloth using vinegar or a household cleaner. To reduce the risk of electric shock, never immerse the base in water and *always unplug the unit first*.

Never use a stoneware bowl or cover if it is chipped or scratched. It's easy to buy a new lid from most manufacturers. Many slow cookers now come with plastic lids, which eliminate the chipping problem.

Using your slow cooker

The slow cooker works by simmering food at a constant low temperature. The **Low** setting cooks food at 200° F (90° C), which is below the boiling point, and the **High** setting cooks food at about 300° F (150° C).

Choosing the right cooking temperature. As a general rule, 1 hour of cooking on

High equals 2 to 2 1/2 hours on **Low**. Foods such as pot roasts and stews are best cooked at a **Low** setting to keep them from boiling. Cooking at the higher temperature may result in a slightly tougher cut of meat. Most of the recipes in this book give cooking times for both **High** and **Low** settings. Where only one cooking time is given, I recommend that it is the one you use. This is especially important for appetizers and desserts where overcooking or undercooking can be an issue.

In fact, since any type of recipe can be overcooked in the slow cooker, it's always best to follow my recommended cooking times. If you start a recipe on **High** and you think you have longer to wait to eat than originally planned, reduce the temperature to **Low**. This will keep food at the right serving temperature without the risk of overcooking.

If the slow cooker will be unattended all day, I recommend cooking on **Low** instead of **High**. At this temperature, the slow cooker cooks food so gently that a few extra hours need not be of concern. Try not to let the cooked food stand longer than 2 hours. Also keep in mind that cooking times are *guidelines* – each slow cooker varies and power fluctuations may occur. After using your slow cooker for a while, you will learn what to expect. In testing the recipes for this book, I used six different types of slow cookers and encountered a considerable range of cooking times. But eventually, I was able to determine what to expect from which slow cooker, and so will you.

Keep in mind that many things can affect how quickly a recipe will cook. Meat should be lean and well trimmed. Too much fat in the cooking liquid will raise its temperature, causing the meat to become overcooked. Browning the meat first will help to reduce its fat content.

Size of food pieces will also affect the cooking time. Food cut into smaller pieces will cook faster than whole roasts or poultry.

Preparing recipes the night before.
Many of the recipes in this book can be made ahead so they're ready to start cooking when you leave for work in the morning – and will be finished when you return home. These are marked with the Night Before symbol ⬤, indicating that the recipe can be assembled in the stoneware insert and refrigerated overnight. If there are any exceptions, such as ingredients that need to be added later, they will be noted on the recipe. The next day, place the stoneware in the slow cooker and cook as directed. The food does not need to come to room temperature before cooking.

Any recipe using meat, whether chunks or ground, can be prepared in advance, provided you brown the meat first. Do not prepare any poultry dish in advance if raw poultry is placed over raw vegetables and left to sit for 12 to 24 hours. For added convenience, you may want to purchase an electrical timer (the kind you use to control your house lights) if you are planning to be away from home for the entire day. Place *refrigerated* food in the slow cooker and set the timer to start 2 hours later (1 hour if it's poultry). You might want to test this method while you are at home. If you try it while you're away and it doesn't work, coming home to an uncooked dinner will be rather unpleasant.

Other variables affecting cooking time.
At higher altitudes (above 3500 ft), cooking may take longer. Extreme humidity can also affect the cooking time. Power fluctuations, which are commonplace everywhere, do not have a noticeable effect on most appliances, but can slightly alter the cooking times with a slow cooker. Keep these things in mind if you find your food is not cooked in the recommended time. You will learn through experience whether to use the shorter or longer time given.

Techniques for slow cooker success

In order to get optimum results from your slow cooker, there are a few things you should consider before getting started.

Browning and broiling. Be sure to brown chunks of meat such as stewing beef and roasts or broil cuts such as pork and beef ribs, before adding to the slow cooker. This not only helps to eliminate additional fat, it will also help to enhance the flavor of the recipe. When cooking meat in the slow cooker, a lot of juices are collected, and steam accumulates. Since it cannot escape as it rises, the steam collects under the lid of the slow cooker, dripping back down into the cooking liquid, making these juices more watery and diluted, and affecting the flavor. Browning and broiling meat first helps to enhance the overall flavor of the dish.

Dredging. Since cooking liquids are diluted in slow cooking, they need to be reduced or thickened in order to intensify their flavor. For soups and stews that require thickening, I prefer to dredge the meat first in seasoned flour before browning. This

13

means you don't have to add a thickening agent at the end of cooking, and you'll have less chance of ending up with lumpy gravy. However, if you are assembling the dish to be refrigerated overnight and don't have time to dredge and brown the meat right away, a flour paste can be added for thickening during the last 25 to 30 minutes of cooking time. Combine 1/4 cup (50 mL) flour with 1/4 cup (50 mL) water, stirring well to eliminate lumps; add directly to the slow cooker, stirring to mix well. Replace the lid and increase the temperature to **High**. Soups, stews and gravies will thicken quite nicely using this method. In some recipes, the gravy or sauce is prepared simply by puréeing the cooking liquid and vegetables.

Cooking poultry. Poultry is one of the easiest things to overcook in the slow cooker. In order to achieve great results, here are a few guidelines to remember.

To improve the flavor, texture and appearance of the recipe, it is best to leave the skin on during slow cooking, then remove it before serving. The best cuts of chicken and turkey for slow cooking are thighs. You can use breasts if you prefer, but you'll need to watch them more carefully to avoid overcooking – about 4 1/2 to 5 hours on **Low** will be sufficient. If you are using a whole cut-up chicken in a recipe, remember that the dark meat takes longer to cook than the white meat, so it's best to place the dark meat on the bottom of the slow cooker, stacking the white meat on the top. As the cooking liquid heats up, it will cook the dark meat first and the white meat later.

A whole chicken can be awkward to cook if you have a 2 1/2- to 3 1/2-quart round slow cooker. It will have to be tilted on its side to fit. (One exception is the DRUNKEN ROAST CHICKEN, which is trussed before placing in the slow cooker so it won't fall apart when it is removed.) It may be easier to cut up a whole chicken into 10 pieces: 2 drumsticks, 2 thighs, 2 wings, 2 breasts and the back chopped into 2 pieces. Turkey thighs and drumsticks are ideal choices to use for poultry in recipes in this book, yielding juicy, tender results.

Pot roasting. Next to a delicious stew, there is nothing more satisfying that a succulent roast, braised in a savory liquid. The slow cooker is ideal for pot roasting and I often prepare this for a Sunday-night dinner, just like my grandmother used to do.

For best results, cook the roast on **Low**. Cooking on **High** can boil the meat and make it tough. Keep in mind that the more marbling (or fat) the meat has, the less liquid you will need. I prefer using a cross-rib or blade beef roast for recipes such as HOMESTYLE POT ROAST or MEDITERRANEAN POT ROAST because they are tender and juicy and slice well. It is best to brown the roast first on all sides in a large Dutch oven or skillet. COMFORTING SHREDDED BEEF uses a sirloin tip roast, which is easily shredded to make PHILLY BEEF WRAPS. A boneless pork shoulder butt roast makes an excellent choice for SOUTHERN BARBECUED PORK ON A BUN or ROAST PORK WITH TANGY CRANBERRY SAUCE since these are less tender cuts of pork and are ideally suited to slow cooking. If you choose a boneless pork loin roast, reduce the cooking time to approximately 5 to 6 hours, since this cut can easily become overcooked.

If you are adding vegetables to the roast, I recommend adding a small amount of liquid to properly soften them. Root vegetables often take longer to cook than meat, so cut sturdy veggies like carrots, potatoes and turnips into small bite-size pieces. Place them in the bottom of the stoneware bowl, add meat and liquid and keep the vegetables submerged in the liquid for uniform cooking.

Low-fat cooking. The slow cooker is a natural for low-fat cooking because you add very little additional fat, if any, to the cooking process. Meat should be trimmed of all visible fat before cooking. (This reduces the fat you eat, and ensures that extra fat doesn't have the undesirable effect of making the food cook faster.) You should also broil beef, pork ribs and chicken wings to remove unnecessary fat before placing them in the slow cooker. When cooking well-marbled roasts it's a good idea to place the onions on the bottom of the slow cooker and place the meat over top. This way the meat will not sit and cook in the fat. If you have a trivet that will fit inside your slow cooker, place the roast on it.

When browning meat or poultry before adding to the slow cooker, try to use a nonstick skillet sprayed with vegetable spray. And as you would normally do, skim any excess fat from the surface of the cooking liquid before serving. Cook chicken with the skin on, since this will help to keep it moist. Then, to cut the fat, remove the skin before serving.

Keeping the lid on! Since the slow cooker works by simmering food at a constant low temperature, it is extremely important to cook with the lid on. Removing the lid dur-ing cooking will result in heat loss (which the slow cooker can't quickly recover) and cause the cooking time to be extended. Lift the lid only when it's time to check for doneness or when stirring is recommended. If you do lift the lid you will need to add about 20 minutes additional cooking time for every time you do so. For recipes in this book where stirring is recommended, the necessary additional cooking time has already been taken into consideration.

If a recipe produces too much liquid at the end of the cooking time, remove the cover, turn to **High** and reduce the liquid for 30 to 45 minutes. Alternatively, you can remove the solid contents of the slow cooker with a slotted spoon and keep them warm in the oven. Pour the cooking liquid into a saucepan and reduce on the stovetop, over high heat, until the sauce has reached the desired consistency.

How much food should you cook at one time? For the slow cooker to work most efficiently, it is important to keep the stoneware insert bowl two-thirds to three-quarters full. Larger cuts of meat should be completely covered with liquid to ensure even cooking. If it is not completely covered, turn the meat over two or three times during the cooking process to ensure any exposed portions do not dry out. Keep in mind that as food cooks and releases its juices, liquid will accumulate in the slow cooker, helping to keep the meat well braised. You should leave a 2-inch (5 cm) space between the top of the stoneware insert and food so that the recipe can come to a simmer.

How to adapt other recipes to the slow cooker. You can tailor any main-dish recipe to suit your own preferences. Here are a few hints to keep in mind.

• Since there is little evaporation in a slow cooker, reduce liquid by about one half when adapting a conventional recipe.

• Vegetables tend to cook more slowly than meat. To avoid undercooked vegetables place vegetables on the bottom and around the sides of the cooker and place the meat on top. Since smaller pieces cook faster than large chunks, cut carrots, potatoes and turnip into small bite-size portions and keep them submerged in the cooking liquid to ensure uniform cooking. Potatoes can be scrubbed, but it is not necessary to peel them; leaving them unpeeled helps them to retain their shape and color in the cooking liquid.

• Add tender vegetables, like peas and snow peas, and strongly flavored vegetables, like broccoli, Brussels sprouts, cauliflower and greens (kale and chard), in the last 15 to 60 minutes. Frozen vegetables, like peas and corn, should be added during the last 15 to 30 minutes. Eggplant should be parboiled or sautéed first to eliminate any bitter flavor.

• Dried beans must be softened completely before adding to any recipe. Sugar and acid have a hardening effect on beans and will prevent softening. See additional information about cooking with dried beans in Chapter 3.

• Some recipe ingredients – such as pasta, seafood, milk, cream and sour cream – are not suited for extended cooking in the slow cooker. They should be added during the last hour of cooking time.

• Cook pasta to the tender-but-firm stage before adding to the slow cooker.

Uncooked rice can be added to the slow cooker, but you will want to add 1/4 cup (50 mL) extra liquid per 1/4 cup (50 mL) rice. Use long grain converted rice for the best results in all-day cooking. The process by which converted rice is made, helps to keep the kernels from sticking together, resulting in an evenly cooked product.

Following is a chart for adapting some of your favorite recipes to the slow cooker. Keep in mind that these times are approximate and you will be the best judge of when your food is tender and completely cooked.

If recipe says	Cook in slow cooker
15 to 30 minutes	1 1/2 to 2 hours on **High** 4 to 6 hours on **Low**
35 to 45 minutes	3 to 4 hours on **High** 6 to 10 hours on **Low**
50 minutes to 3 hours	4 to 6 hours on **High** 8 to 18 hours on **Low**

Rival Cooking Chart Times

Most meat and vegetable combinations will require at least 8 hours on **Low**.

Ensuring food safety with your slow cooker

Generally, foods cooked in a slow cooker reach their internal cooked temperature quickly enough to inhibit bacterial growth. To qualify as safe, a slow cooker must be able to cook slowly enough for unattended cooking, yet with sufficient heat to keep food above the danger zone (180° F [80° C]). If you have an old slow cooker gathering dust and you aren't sure if it is still safe to use, try this:

1. Fill cooker with 8 cups (2 L) water.

2. Cover and heat on **Low** for 8 hours.

3. Check the water temperature with an accurate cooking thermometer. Do this quickly, since removing the lid for an extended time can drop the temperature 10 to 15 degrees.

4. The thermometer should read about 185° F (85° C). A higher temperature indicates that a product cooked for 8 hours, without stirring, would be overcooked. A lower temperature suggests that the slow cooker does not generate sufficient heat to avoid potential food-safety problems.

Even if your slow cooker is functioning properly, it is important to follow a few guidelines for optimum safety. First and foremost, always start with fresh or thawed (not frozen) food, particularly meats. Frozen vegetables, such as green peas and corn, can be added at the end of the cooking time since they have been par-cooked and flash frozen by the manufacturer. If using ground meat – including beef, pork, turkey or chicken – always brown it in a skillet before adding to the slow cooker with other ingredients. If you can, try cooking meat at **High** first for 1 hour, then reduce to **Low** for the remainder of the cooking time. When cooking soups and stews, leave a 2-inch (5 cm) head-space between the top of the stoneware and the lid so that the recipe can come to a simmer. If cooking a soup or stew on **High**, keep an eye on its progress, since it may come to a boil when cooked at this temperature. Wrist burns can occur when lifting the lid, so always open it away from you to avoid being burned by the steam.

What to do with leftovers. Foods should not be reheated in a slow cooker. Just as in conventional cooking, any leftover food should be removed from the slow cooker and stored in plastic containers for up to 2 days in the refrigerator, or frozen for later use. (Most of the recipes in this book freeze well and can be reheated.) Leftovers can be thawed or reheated in a conventional or microwave oven, or on the stovetop.

Appetizers & Beverages

Bacon-Onion Chip Dip

**Makes about
3 cups (750 mL)**

Why serve the store-bought variety when you can put out a pot of this warm dip? Try it with potato chips or, for a change, crunchy pretzels or sesame sticks. Everyone will be looking for more.

A mini (1-quart) slow cooker is ideal for entertaining. It is inexpensive and handy to have on hand for warm dips and spreads.

☾ NIGHT BEFORE

The ingredients for this dip can be prepared up to 24 hours in advance and refrigerated. Spoon into prepared slow cooker and heat as directed. To reheat leftovers, microwave at Medium for 2 to 3 minutes. Stir before serving.

SLOW COOKER STONEWARE INSERT, LIGHTLY GREASED

6	slices bacon, finely chopped	6
1	pkg (8 oz [250 g]) light cream cheese, softened	1
1 cup	light sour cream	250 mL
1/2 cup	shredded old Cheddar cheese	125 mL
2	green onions, finely chopped	2
	Potato chips or crackers	

1. In a nonstick skillet over medium-high heat, cook bacon 7 to 8 minutes or until crisp. Transfer to a paper towel-lined plate to drain.
2. In a bowl combine cream cheese, cooked bacon, sour cream, Cheddar cheese and green onions. Mix well and transfer to prepared slow cooker.
3. Cover and cook on **High** for 1 hour or until cheese is melted (do not stir). Reduce heat to **Low** until ready to serve.
4. Transfer to a bowl and serve with plain potato chips or as a spread on crackers. Dip will keep well in the refrigerator for several days.

Hot Crab, Artichoke and Jalapeño Spread

**Makes about
3 cups (750 mL)**

This spread is the ultimate winter treat – warm and creamy, with just a nip of spicy heat from the jalapeño peppers. Serve it after skiing, with a basket of breadsticks or crackers.

Both light and regular mayonnaise work well in this recipe. Just be sure that it's real mayonnaise – not whipped-style salad dressing.

You can substitute a 4-oz (113 g) can of well-drained shrimp for crabmeat.

SLOW COOKER STONEWARE INSERT, LIGHTLY GREASED

1 tsp	vegetable oil	5 mL
1	jalapeño pepper, seeded and finely chopped	1
Half	red bell pepper, finely chopped	Half
1	can (14 oz [398 mL]) artichokes, drained and finely chopped	1
1 cup	mayonnaise	250 mL
1/4 cup	freshly grated Parmesan cheese	50 mL
2	green onions, finely chopped	2
2 tsp	lemon juice	10 mL
2 tsp	Worcestershire sauce	10 mL
1/2 tsp	celery seed	2 mL
1	can (6 oz [170 g]) crabmeat, drained	1

1. In a nonstick skillet, heat oil over medium heat. Add jalapeño and red pepper; sauté for 5 minutes or until tender.

2. In a bowl combine artichokes, mayonnaise, Parmesan cheese, green onions, lemon juice, Worcestershire sauce, celery seed, crabmeat and sautéed peppers. Mix well and spoon into prepared slow cooker.

3. Cover and cook on **Low** for 4 to 6 hours or on **High** for 2 to 2 1/2 hours. Do not stir. Alternatively, cook on **High** for 1 1/2 to 2 hours and then reduce to **Low** to keep warm until ready to serve.

Warm-and-Wonderful Seafood Dip

Serves 4 to 6

Less than 5 minutes to prepare the ingredients, then a few hours of unattended cooking – that's all you need to make this wonderful dip for vegetables, crackers or thin slices of baguette.

A mini (1-quart) slow cooker is ideal for this recipe; it's just the right size and will keep its contents at the right temperature for serving your guests.

In the unlikely event that you have any leftover dip, don't let it go to waste. It can be refrigerated, then enjoyed the next day; just reheat in the microwave at Medium for 2 to 2 1/2 minutes or until warm. Or, for a tasty lunchtime treat, make a hot seafood wrap: spread leftover dip on a soft flour tortilla; add sliced red bell pepper and cucumber, sprinkle with alfalfa sprouts; roll up the tortilla and serve.

1	pkg (8 oz [250 g]) cream cheese, softened	1
1/2 cup	mayonnaise	125 mL
3	green onions, chopped	3
2	cloves garlic, minced	2
2 tbsp	lemon juice	25 mL
1/4 cup	tomato paste	50 mL
2	cans (each 4 oz [113 g]) tiny shrimp or 2 cans (each 6 oz [170 g]) crabmeat, drained	2
	Salt and pepper	

1. In a bowl, blend together cream cheese, mayonnaise, green onions, garlic, lemon juice and tomato paste. Blend in seafood, mashing with a fork. Season to taste with salt and pepper. (Alternatively, place all ingredients except shrimp in a food processor; pulse 2 or 3 times until mixture is smooth and well blended; add shrimp and pulse once or twice more.) Transfer mixture to slow cooker.

2. Cover and cook on **Low** for 2 to 3 hours or on **High** for 1 to 1 1/2 hours. Set slow cooker to **Low** to keep dip warm until ready to serve with assorted vegetable dippers or crackers.

Just-like-Refried Frijoles Dip

Serves 8 to 10

Contrary to popular belief, refried beans aren't actually fried twice – they're first boiled in a pot of water, then fried in a skillet. And in fact, this "refried" bean dip isn't even fried *once*, but the slow cooker brings out a great "refried" flavor.

TIP

Use any leftover dip to make a delicious burrito: spread dip on a warm tortilla shell; add seasoned ground beef, chopped lettuce, tomato, salsa and sour cream; roll up and serve with extra salsa.

SLOW COOKER STONEWARE INSERT, LIGHTLY GREASED

2 tsp	vegetable oil	10 mL
1	medium onion, finely chopped	1
4	cloves garlic, minced	4
1 1/2 tbsp	chili powder	20 mL
1 tsp	ground cumin	5 mL
2	cans (each 19 oz [540 mL]) pinto or Romano beans, rinsed and drained	2
3/4 cup	hot water	175 mL
1/2 tsp	salt	2 mL
1 cup	grated Cheddar cheese	250 mL
1/2 cup	light sour cream	125 mL
	Chopped green onions	
	Tortilla chips	

1. In a small skillet, heat oil over medium heat. Add onion, garlic, chili powder and cumin; sauté for 5 minutes or until onion is translucent and tender. Set aside.

2. In a bowl with a potato masher (or in a blender or food processor), combine beans and hot water until smooth. Add seasoned onion mixture and salt; blend and mix well. Transfer to prepared slow cooker.

3. Cover and cook on **Low** for 3 to 4 hours or on **High** for 1 to 2 hours. Reduce heat to **Low**. Sprinkle with Cheddar cheese and spoon sour cream in center of dip. Cover and cook another 20 minutes or until cheese has melted. Set slow cooker to **Low** to keep dip warm until ready to serve. Garnish dip with chopped green onions and serve with tortilla chips.

Savory Meatballs with Cranberry Sauce

Serves 10 to 15 as an appetizer or 6 to 8 as a main dish

Portable and delicious, meatballs make the perfect party food. This dish can be prepared, brought to the party, and ultimately served in the slow cooker.

MAKE AHEAD

These meatballs can be made up to 1 day ahead and stored in the refrigerator or frozen for up to 2 months. To freeze, place meatballs in a single layer on baking sheet. When frozen, place in a storage container. To assemble dish, place meatballs in slow cooker. Add sauce and heat on **Low** for 6 to 10 hours.

MEATBALLS

2 lbs	lean ground beef or pork	1 kg
2	eggs, lightly beaten	2
1 cup	fine dry breadcrumbs	250 mL
1/2 tsp	salt	2 mL
1/2 tsp	black pepper	2 mL
1/2 tsp	garlic powder	2 mL
1/2 tsp	paprika	2 mL

CRANBERRY SAUCE

1 cup	ketchup	250 mL
1 cup	tomato juice	250 mL
1	can (14 oz [398 mL]) whole-berry cranberry sauce *or* 1 1/2 cups (375 mL) homemade cranberry sauce	1
1	medium onion, finely chopped	1
1 tbsp	brown sugar	15 mL
1 tsp	ground ginger	5 mL

1. Meatballs: In a large bowl, combine beef, eggs, breadcrumbs, salt, pepper, garlic powder and paprika; work mixture with your hands until thoroughly blended. Form into 1-inch (2.5 cm) balls. Place on baking sheet. Bake in preheated oven, uncovered, for 18 to 20 minutes or until nicely browned. Drain off any accumulated juices and transfer to slow cooker.

2. Cranberry sauce: In a bowl combine ketchup, tomato juice, cranberry sauce, onion, sugar and ginger; mix well and pour over meatballs. Cover and cook on **Low** for 6 to 10 hours or on **High** for 3 to 4 hours.

3. Meatballs can be served directly from the slow cooker or transferred to a bowl and garnished with freshly chopped parsley. If serving as a main dish, serve over hot buttered noodles.

Oriental Chicken Wings

Serves 8 to 10 as an appetizer or 4 to 6 as a main course

TIP

This is one of my favorite dishes for the buffet table. But you can also enjoy it as a main course served over steamed rice.

Buy pre-separated wings for faster preparation.

This recipe can easily be doubled for a larger crowd.

Wings are also tasty cold, so refrigerate any leftovers to enjoy the next day as a snack.

PREHEAT BROILER

BAKING PAN, FOIL-LINED

2 lbs	chicken wings, tips removed and split in half at joint	1 kg
1/2 cup	cider vinegar	125 mL
1/2 cup	brown sugar	125 mL
1/4 cup	soya sauce	50 mL
1/4 cup	water	50 mL
4	cloves garlic, minced	4
1 tsp	lemon juice	5 mL
1 tsp	ground ginger	5 mL
1/2 tsp	dry mustard	2 mL
	Sesame seeds (optional)	

1. Arrange split chicken wings on prepared baking pan. Gently cook wings under preheated broiler (6 inches [15 cm] from heat) for 10 to 20 minutes or until golden, turning wings once during cooking. Transfer wings to slow cooker. Discard foil and drippings.

2. In a bowl combine vinegar, sugar, soya sauce, water, garlic, lemon juice, ginger and mustard; mix well and pour over wings.

3. Cover and cook on **Low** for 4 to 5 hours or on **High** for 2 to 3 hours, turning 2 or 3 times during cooking.

4. Wings can be served directly from the slow cooker, or arranged on a serving platter. If desired, garnish with a sprinkling of sesame seeds.

Peking Pork Bites

Makes about 24

PREHEAT OVEN TO 350° F (180° C)
BAKING SHEET, FOIL-LINED

You won't be able to stop at just a few of these tasty bites. The sauce makes them irresistible.

TIP

Hoisin sauce is a kind of Chinese "ketchup." It has a sweet but tangy flavor and is available in the Oriental foods section of the supermarket.

MAKE AHEAD

Pork bites can be cooked up to a day ahead and stored in the refrigerator (or frozen for up to 2 months). To freeze, place in a single layer on a baking sheet and place in the freezer. When frozen, transfer to covered containers or resealable freezer bags. Thaw before placing in sauce.

PORK BITES

1 lb	lean ground pork	500 g
1/2 cup	fine dry breadcrumbs	125 mL
2 tbsp	hoisin sauce	25 mL
2	cloves garlic, minced	2
1	green onion, minced	1
1	egg, lightly beaten	1

PEKING SAUCE

3/4 cup	hoisin sauce	175 mL
3/4 cup	redcurrant jelly	175 mL
1 tbsp	lemon juice	15 mL
2	cloves garlic, minced	2
1 tbsp	grated ginger root (or 1 tsp [5 mL] ground ginger)	15 mL
	Sesame seeds	

1. Pork Bites: In a bowl combine ground pork, breadcrumbs, hoisin sauce, garlic, green onion and egg; mix well. Shape into 1-inch (2.5 cm) balls.

2. Place meatballs on prepared baking sheet and bake in preheated oven for 20 minutes or until browned. Transfer to slow cooker. Discard foil and drippings.

3. Peking Sauce: In a 4-cup (1 L) measure or bowl, combine hoisin sauce, redcurrant jelly, lemon juice, garlic and ginger; mix well and pour over meatballs. Cover and cook on **Low** for 5 to 6 hours or on **High** for 2 to 3 hours.

4. Meatballs can be served directly from the slow cooker or arranged on a serving platter and sprinkled with sesame seeds.

Novel Curried Walnuts

**Makes about
4 cups (1 L)**

These little nibblers have an exotic spicy flavor. I like to snack on them as I read a novel – hence the name! You can't stop at one.

TIP

Storing nuts. Because of their high fat content, nuts (and particularly walnuts) will quickly become rancid unless kept in the refrigerator or freezer. If possible, taste before buying. If you do store them in the freezer, there's no need to defrost before use.

1/4 cup	melted butter or margarine	50 mL
2 tbsp	curry powder	25 mL
2 tbsp	Worcestershire sauce	25 mL
2 tsp	salt	10 mL
1 tsp	onion powder	5 mL
4 cups	walnut halves	1 L

1. In a 1-cup (250 mL) measure, combine butter, curry powder, Worcestershire sauce, salt and onion powder; mix well. Place walnuts in slow cooker and pour over butter mixture; toss nuts to coat.

2. Cover and cook on **High**, stirring 2 or 3 times during cooking, for 2 hours or until nuts are browned and fragrant.

3. Cool and store in a tightly sealed container for up to 3 weeks.

Zesty Nuts and Birdseed

**Makes about
2 1/2 cups (625 mL)**

This tasty snack is definitely
not for the birds! It will keep
in an airtight container for up
to 2 weeks.

VARIATION

Sunflower seeds can be
replaced with pumpkin seeds
or dried soybeans. Look for
them in the bulk-food department of supermarkets or in
health food stores.

2 cups	unsalted cashews, pecans or almonds	500 mL
1/2 cup	unsalted sunflower seeds	125 mL
2 tbsp	melted butter or margarine	25 mL
1/4 cup	soya sauce	50 mL
1/2 tsp	salt	2 mL
1/4 tsp	hot pepper sauce	1 mL

1. Place nuts and sunflower seeds in slow cooker. Add melted butter, soya sauce, salt and hot pepper sauce; toss nuts to coat with butter mixture. Cover and cook on **High** for 2 hours, stirring frequently (about 4 or 5 times). Allow to cool before nibbling.

Spicy Popcorn with Nuts

**Makes about
3 cups (750 mL)**

If you are anything like me, there's nothing quite so satisfying as a little snack at about 8:00 at night, after the children have gone to bed. My husband and I enjoy this tasty mixture, which combines crunchy popcorn and savory spiced nuts.

TIP

Enjoy with a cold beer or herbal tea.

This mixture stores well in a tightly sealed plastic container for up to 1 week.

1/4 cup	popping corn	50 mL
1/2 cup	peanuts, salted or unsalted	125 mL
1/2 cup	pecan halves	125 mL
2 tbsp	melted butter	25 mL
2 tsp	chili powder	10 mL
1 tsp	garlic powder	5 mL
1/2 tsp	ground cumin	2 mL
1/2 tsp	salt	2 mL

1. In a hot-air popper or large saucepan with a tight-fitting lid, pop corn. Place in a large bowl with peanuts and pecans.
2. In a small bowl, combine butter, chili powder, garlic powder, ground cumin and salt; mix well. Drizzle over popcorn and nuts, tossing to coat well.
3. Transfer mixture to slow cooker. Cover and cook on **High** for 2 hours, stirring once or twice during cooking time. Allow to cool slightly before serving.

Winter Trail Mix

**Makes about
6 cups (1.5 L)**

Chunks of caramelized
pecan crunch combine with
dried apricots and cherries to
make an irresistible tote-
along snack. You can toss
together a batch in no time.
Store in a tightly sealed
plastic container and it will
keep fresh for up to 1 week.

VARIATION

For a delicious bridge mix,
try adding chocolate-covered
cherries or blueberries to the
cooked, cooled mixture .

BAKING SHEET, FOIL-LINED

1/2 cup	granulated sugar	125 mL
2 tbsp	melted butter or margarine	25 mL
1 1/2 tbsp	water	20 mL
1/2 tsp	vanilla	2 mL
1 1/2 cups	pecan halves	375 mL
1 cup	whole almonds	250 mL
2 tsp	finely grated orange zest	25 mL
1 1/2 cups	sesame sticks *or* pretzel sticks	375 mL
1 cup	dried apricots	250 mL
1 cup	dried cherries *or* dried cranberries	250 mL

1. In a small glass measure, combine sugar, butter, water and vanilla. Place pecans and almonds in slow cooker; pour butter mixture over nuts and toss to coat.

2. Cover and cook on **High**, stirring frequently, for 2 to 3 hours or until sugar mixture is golden brown and nuts are toasted. Stir in orange zest; toss to coat and turn out onto prepared baking sheet. Set aside to cool.

3. In a large bowl or airtight storage container, combine nut mixture with sesame sticks, apricots and cherries.

Apple Cinnamon Sippers

Makes 8 cups (2 L)

CHEESECLOTH AND ELASTIC BAND OR KITCHEN TWINE
PREHEAT OVEN TO 350° F (180° C)
13- BY 9-INCH (3 L) BAKING DISH

2	cinnamon sticks	2
1 tsp	whole cloves	5 mL
1 tsp	whole allspice berries	5 mL
8 cups	apple cider	2 L
1/2 cup	packed brown sugar	125 mL
1	orange, sliced	1
3	large baking apples, cored (optional)	3

1. Place cinnamon, cloves and allspice on a double thickness of cheesecloth. Bring up corners of cloth and tie with an elastic band or kitchen twine to form a bag.

2. Combine cider and brown sugar in slow cooker, stirring until sugar dissolves. Add spice bag. Place orange slices on top. Cover and cook on **Low** for 2 to 5 hours or until hot. Remove spice bag and discard.

3. Optional: For a decorative touch, cut apples in half crosswise and place, cut-side down, in baking dish. Bake in preheated oven for 25 minutes or until apple halves are fork tender. Place apples in punch, floating skin-side up.

Caramel Hot Chocolate

Serves 10 to 12

A sip or two of this cold-weather favorite is bound to produce warm smiles, especially when its secret ingredient – the chocolate caramel candy bar – is dissolved.

TIP

I use dry skim milk powder in this recipe because it doesn't curdle and holds up well during long cooking. You will be surprised at how creamy this beverage is.

VARIATION

You can substitute mini marshmallows for the whipped cream. For an adult version, try adding a shot of Irish Cream liqueur or brandy to the mug.

4 cups	dry skim milk powder	1 L
3/4 cup	cocoa	75 mL
1/2 cup	granulated sugar	125 mL
8 cups	water	2 L
1	chocolate-covered caramel-filled candy bar (about 2 oz [50 g])	1
	Whipped cream	
	Grated chocolate (optional)	

1. Add skim milk powder, cocoa and sugar to slow cooker; stir to combine. Slowly add water, whisking constantly to avoid lumps.
2. Cover and cook on **Low** for 4 to 5 hours or until hot.
3. Break chocolate bar into pieces and add to hot chocolate, stirring until completely melted. To serve, ladle into mugs and garnish with whipped cream and grated chocolate.

WINTER TRAIL MIX (PAGE 30) WITH TANGY WINTERBERRY WARMERS (PAGE 35) ➤

Hot Buttered Rum

Serves 6 to 8

TIP

After a day on the icy slopes this drink is sure to warm everyone to their toes. Serve in mugs garnished with whole cinnamon sticks.

Amber or dark rum is the best choice for this winter warmer; white rum tends to give it a metallic flavor.

CHEESECLOTH AND ELASTIC BAND OR KITCHEN TWINE

2 cups	packed brown sugar	500 mL
1/2 cup	butter	125 mL
Pinch	salt	Pinch
1/2 tsp	ground nutmeg	2 mL
6 cups	hot water	1.5 L
3 or 4	whole cloves	3 or 4
3	cinnamon sticks	3
2 cups	amber or dark rum	500 mL

1. In slow cooker, combine sugar, butter, salt and nutmeg. Pour in hot water, stirring until butter is melted and sugar dissolved.
2. Wrap cloves and cinnamon in a cheesecloth bag, secure with an elastic band and place in slow cooker.
3. Cover and cook on **Low** for 4 to 10 hours. Add rum just before serving.

◄ CARROT ORANGE BISQUE (PAGE 45)

Mulled Red Wine

Serves 12

Any time you are feeling a chill, there's nothing better than a warm mug of mulled red wine.

TIP

Don't let the citrus peel float in the wine longer than 4 hours or it will start to taste bitter.

CHEESECLOTH AND ELASTIC BAND OR KITCHEN TWINE

2	bottles (each 25 oz [750 mL]) red wine	2
2 cups	orange juice	500 mL
2 cups	pineapple juice	500 mL
1/2 cup	granulated sugar	125 mL
1	lemon, sliced	1
1	orange, sliced	1
2	cinnamon sticks	2
4	whole cloves	4
4	whole allspice berries	4

1. In slow cooker, combine wine, orange juice, pineapple juice, sugar, lemon slices and orange slices. Wrap cinnamon sticks, cloves and allspice in a piece of cheesecloth and secure with an elastic band. Float in wine mixture.

2. Cover and cook on **Low** for 4 hours or until hot. Remove cheesecloth packet and citrus slices. Leave temperature set on **Low**. Slow cooker will keep punch at proper serving temperature for up to 4 hours.

Tangy Winterberry Warmers

Makes about 12 cups (3 L)

This non-alcoholic winter warmer is perfect after a family day outdoors.

TIP

For a fruity alcoholic version, add a shot of peach or apple schnapps to your mug.

Spice sachets are a perfect holiday gift that even the kids can make. Inside squares of cheesecloth place 2 cinnamon sticks about 4 inches (10 cm) long, 15 allspice berries, and 2 tsp (10 mL) whole cloves. Secure with an elastic band. Attach a handwritten recipe card and tie it up with a pretty red satin ribbon.(Don't forget to make one for yourself!) Use this packet in teas or punches that call for a spice sachet.

CHEESECLOTH BAG AND ELASTIC BAND OR KITCHEN TWINE

6 cups	cranberry juice	1.5 L
2	cans (each 12.5 oz [355 mL]) frozen lemonade concentrate, thawed	2
2 cups	water	500 mL
2	cinnamon sticks	2
1/2 tsp	ground allspice	2 mL
1	lemon, cut into thick slices	1

1. In slow cooker, combine cranberry juice, lemonade concentrate and water.

2. Wrap cinnamon and allspice in a cheesecloth bag and secure with elastic band. Add to juice mixture. Float lemon slices in juice.

3. Cover and cook on **Low** for 4 hours or until hot. Remove cheesecloth packet. Leave temperature set on **Low**. Slow cooker will keep punch at the proper serving temperature for up to 4 hours.

Hot 'n' Spicy Winter Punch

Serves 6 to 8

CHEESECLOTH, ELASTIC BAND AND KITCHEN TWINE

8 cups	cranberry-apple cocktail	2 L
1 tsp	lemon juice	5 mL
4 oz	cinnamon red hots *or* cinnamon heart candy	125 g
2	cinnamon sticks	2
16	whole cloves	16
1 cup	white rum	250 mL

TIP

If you have difficulty finding cranberry-apple cocktail, use 6 cups (1.5 L) apple juice and 2 cups (500 mL) cranberry cocktail.

1. In slow cooker, combine cranberry-apple cocktail, lemon juice and cinnamon red hots.
2. Wrap cinnamon sticks and cloves in a cheesecloth bag; secure with an elastic band and place in slow cooker. Cover and heat on **Low** for 4 to 6 hours or on **High** for 1 to 2 hours.
3. Stir in rum just before serving.

Soups

Autumn Celebration Soup

Serves 4 to 6

Here's a flavorful harvest soup that makes a great starter for Thanksgiving or Christmas dinner – or, served with crusty bread, a hearty lunch on its own. It gets its delicious autumn feel from the surprising combination of rutabagas, caraway seeds and paprika.

For a decorative touch, ladle soup into serving bowls. Dollop sour cream over top and, using a skewer, draw a design on the surface of the soup. Garnish with crisp bacon bits, if desired.

Rutabagas are a yellow-fleshed relative of the turnip – although they are larger and slightly sweeter. Rutabagas and turnips (you can use either in this recipe) will keep all winter in a cold cellar. Remember to remove the waxy outer skin before cooking.

MAKE AHEAD

The purée and vegetable stock can be prepared in advance and refrigerated for up to 3 days or frozen for up to 1 month. Reheat previously thawed purée in slow cooker and add thawed stock and cream as directed.

1 lb	rutabaga, peeled and cut into 1-inch (2.5 cm) cubes (about 4 cups [1 L])	500 g
1	onion, chopped	1
1	potato, peeled and cubed	1
2	carrots, peeled and chopped	2
1 cup	chicken stock	250 mL
1/2 cup	dry white wine	125 mL
2 cups	water	500 mL
2 tbsp	brown sugar	25 mL
2 tsp	caraway seeds	10 mL
1 tbsp	paprika	15 mL
2 cups	milk or light (5%) cream	500 mL
	Sour cream	
	Crisp bacon bits (optional)	

1. In slow cooker, combine rutabaga, onion, potato, carrots, stock, wine, water, sugar, caraway seeds and paprika. Cover and cook on **Low** for 10 to 12 hours or on **High** for 6 to 8 hours, until vegetables are tender.

2. Strain the vegetables, reserving stock. In a blender or food processor, purée vegetables in batches. Transfer back to slow cooker; add reserved stock and milk. Heat on **Low** for 25 to 30 minutes or until warmed through.

3. Spoon soup into individual bowls and garnish with dollops of sour cream and a sprinkle of bacon bits.

Easy Bean and Barley Soup

Serves 6 to 8

1	can (14 oz [398 mL]) beans in tomato sauce	1
2	medium potatoes, peeled and finely chopped	2
1	stalk celery, finely chopped	1
1	large onion, finely chopped	1
2	leeks (white parts only) trimmed, well rinsed and thinly sliced	2
2	medium carrots, diced	2
6 cups	beef stock	1.5 L
1/2 cup	pearl or pot barley, rinsed	125 mL
Pinch	ground nutmeg	Pinch

1. In slow cooker, stir together beans, potatoes, celery, onion, leeks, carrots, stock, barley and nutmeg.
2. Cover and cook on **Low** for 8 to 10 hours or on **High** for 4 to 6 hours, until vegetables are tender and soup is bubbling.

TIP

This is my idea of a no-fuss family meal – and the kids love it! I like to know that I can reach into the cupboard, pull out some convenient canned products and whip together a healthy soup in no time.

VARIATION

For a wonderfully rich, sweet broth, try beans in tomato sauce with maple syrup. Or add 2 tbsp (25 mL) maple syrup to the ingredients.

As an added treat for kids, chop up some cooked hot dogs and add to the soup. Now they can eat "Wieners and Beaners."

NIGHT BEFORE

This dish can be completely assembled the night before. Follow preparation directions and refrigerate overnight in the slow cooker stoneware. The next day, place stoneware in slow cooker and continue cooking as directed.

Hearty Beef Goulash

Serves 6 to 8

This is one of those soups that some might call a stew. Its rich, beefy taste has lots of old-fashioned appeal.

TIP

For a great light meal, serve with thick crusty rolls and a tossed salad.

This soup makes enough for leftovers. It will freeze well, so ladle into freezer-safe containers, label and store up to 3 months. Add 1/2 cup (125 mL) water to soup when reheating.

🌙 NIGHT BEFORE

This soup can be completely assembled up to 12 to 24 hours in advance. Follow preparation directions and refrigerate overnight in the slow cooker stoneware. The next day, place stoneware in slow cooker and continue cooking as directed.

1/4 cup	all-purpose flour	50 mL
2 tsp	paprika	10 mL
1 tsp	salt	5 mL
1/2 tsp	black pepper	2 mL
1/2 tsp	dried thyme	2 mL
2 lbs	stewing beef, cut into small cubes	1 kg
1 tbsp	vegetable oil	15 mL
3 cups	beef stock	750 mL
1	small can (7.5 oz [213 mL]) tomato sauce	1
2	onions, chopped	2
2	cloves garlic	2
1 cup	diced carrots (about 2 medium)	250 mL
1 cup	chopped celery (about 2 stalks)	250 mL
2	potatoes, peeled and diced	2
1	bay leaf	1

1. In a bowl or plastic bag, combine flour, paprika, salt, pepper and thyme. In batches, add beef to flour mixture and toss to coat. Transfer to a plate. In a large skillet, heat half the oil over medium-high heat. Add beef in batches and cook, adding more oil as needed, until browned all over. With a slotted spoon, transfer beef to slow cooker.

2. Add stock, tomato sauce, onions, garlic, carrots, celery, potatoes and bay leaf to slow cooker. Cover and cook on **Low** for 8 to 10 hours or on **High** for 4 to 6 hours, until vegetables are tender. Remove and discard bay leaf before serving.

Boxing Day Turkey Soup

Serves 4 to 6

Here's a rich and delicious solution to an age-old post Christmas problem – "What to do with the leftover turkey?"

TIP

For a creamier version, omit the tomatoes and add 1 can (14 oz [398 mL]) cream-style corn.

For best results with all-day cooking, use long grain converted rice.

MAKE AHEAD

You don't have to wait until Boxing Day to try this delicious soup. I often make stock and freeze it for later use. The meat, removed from the bones, can also be wrapped and frozen for later use. Thaw frozen stock and meat first; add to slow cooker and continue as directed.

6 cups	NO-FUSS TURKEY STOCK (see recipe, page 46) *or* 3 cans (each 10 oz [284 mL]) chicken broth, diluted with equal parts water	1.5 L
2 cups	chopped cooked turkey	500 mL
1	can (19 oz [540 mL]) tomatoes, with juice, chopped	1
2	medium carrots, chopped	2
2	stalks celery, chopped	2
1	medium onion, chopped	1
1/4 cup	long grain converted rice	50 mL
2 tbsp	chopped fresh parsley (or 2 tsp [10mL] dried)	25 mL
1/2 tsp	dried thyme	2 mL
1 1/2 cups	frozen corn kernels	375 mL
	Salt and pepper	

1. In slow cooker, combine stock, turkey, tomatoes, carrots, celery, onion, rice, parsley and thyme.

2. Cover and cook on **Low** for 8 to 10 hours or on **High** for 4 to 6 hours, until vegetables are tender and soup is bubbling. Add corn; cover and cook on **High** for 20 minutes. Season to taste with salt and pepper.

Black Bean Cassoulet Soup

Serves 6 to 8

A traditional French cassoulet is chock-full of beans, chicken, sausage, ham and vegetables. This "bistro-style" soup is much easier to make and has a lot of the same great flavor.

TIP

For a great one-course meal, serve with a tossed salad, lots of crusty French bread and glasses of crisp, cold white wine.

Smoked pork hocks are available in most supermarkets and butcher shops. The hock comes from the pork leg. Hocks make wonderful additions to soups and stews. If you can't find one, use a meaty ham bone instead.

You may want to use the cooking broth and leftover meat from the SLOW COOKER COTTAGE ROLL (see recipe, page 127). Substitute 5 cups (1.25 L) cooking liquid for water and 2 cups (500 mL) meat for the smoked pork hock. Do not add the meat as in Step 1, but after the beans have been puréed.

1	medium onion, diced	1
3	cloves garlic, minced	3
1	smoked pork hock or meaty ham bone (about 2 lbs [1 kg]), outer skin removed	1
6 cups	water	1.5 L
1 tsp	ground cumin	5 mL
1 tsp	dried oregano	5 mL
1	bay leaf	1
1 tsp	salt	5 mL
1/2 tsp	black pepper	2 mL
1	can (19 oz [540 mL]) black beans, rinsed and drained *or* 2 cups (500 mL) cooked black beans, rinsed and drained	1
1 lb	hot Italian sausage, browned and cut into 1-inch (2.5 cm) pieces	500 g
1	red bell pepper, cored, seeded and diced	1
2 tbsp	chopped fresh parsley (or 1 tbsp [15 mL] dried)	25 mL
1 tbsp	dry sherry	15 mL
1 tbsp	brown sugar	15 mL
2 tsp	lemon juice	10 mL
	Sour cream	

1. In slow cooker, combine onion, garlic, smoked pork hock, water, cumin, oregano, bay leaf, salt, pepper and black beans; stir to mix well.

NIGHT BEFORE

This soup can be partially assembled 12 to 24 hours in advance of cooking. Prepare ingredients as directed and refrigerate overnight in slow cooker stoneware. The next day, place stoneware in slow cooker and cook as directed.

2. Cover and cook on **Low** for 8 to 10 hours or on **High** for 4 to 6 hours, until meat is tender. Gently remove the pork hock. Shred the meat and set aside. Remove bay leaf and discard. Transfer 1 cup (250 mL) of bean mixture to a food processor or blender and process until smooth. Return to slow cooker with shredded meat.

3. Add cooked sausage, red pepper, parsley, sherry, brown sugar and lemon juice. Cover and cook on **High** for 1 hour. Ladle soup into individual bowls and serve garnished with a dollop of sour cream.

Caribbean Pepper Pot Soup

Serves 4 to 6

1 tbsp	vegetable oil	15 mL
2 lbs	stewing beef, cut into 1-inch (2.5 cm) cubes	1 kg
1	Scotch Bonnet pepper, seeded and finely chopped *or* 1 tsp (5 mL) hot pepper sauce	1
4	cloves garlic, minced	4
3	sweet potatoes, peeled and cut into 1-inch (2.5 cm) squares	3
2	onions, finely chopped	2
4 cups	beef stock	1 L
1 cup	water	250 mL
1/4 cup	tomato paste	50 mL
1 tsp	dried thyme	5 mL
1 tsp	salt	5 mL
1/2 tsp	black pepper	2 mL
1	red bell pepper, diced	1
1	green pepper, diced	1

1. In a large nonstick skillet, heat oil over medium-high heat. Add beef cubes and Scotch Bonnet pepper and cook until meat is brown on all sides. (If using hot sauce, this is added in Step 4.) With a slotted spoon, transfer meat and pepper to slow cooker.

2. Add garlic, sweet potatoes, onions, stock, water, tomato paste, thyme, salt and pepper to slow cooker; stir to combine.

3. Cover and cook on **Low** for 8 to 10 hours or on **High** for 4 to 6 hours, until vegetables are tender and soup is bubbling.

4. Add red pepper, green pepper and, if using, hot pepper sauce; stir to mix well. Cover and cook on **High** for 20 to 25 minutes before serving.

TIP

This delectable soup, almost a meal in itself, brings home a touch of the West Indies. Make it the centerpiece of a "beat-the-winter-blahs" party: Invite friends over, put on some calypso music, and serve a few tropical drinks to start, then bring on the soup.

Scotch Bonnet peppers are available in supermarkets where West Indian produce is sold. They are reputed to be the hottest peppers in the world – so be sure to wear gloves when chopping and seeding.

If the soup is ready before you are, reduce the slow cooker temperature to **Low**. This will keep the food warm without overcooking.

NIGHT BEFORE

This soup can be completely assembled up to 12 to 24 hours in advance of cooking (but without adding the red and green pepper and hot pepper sauce, if using). Follow preparation directions and refrigerate overnight in the slow cooker stoneware. The next day, place stoneware in slow cooker and continue cooking as directed.

Carrot Orange Bisque

Serves 4

This is a wonderful starter for an elegant meal – or it can be a meal on its own.

TIP

This recipe can easily be doubled, but don't change the quantity of orange zest: it will be too overpowering.

To extract the most juice from oranges, use fruit that has been sitting at room temperature. Roll firmly on a flat surface using the palm of your hand. Or microwave a whole orange on **High** for 30 seconds, and then roll. Juice can be frozen in ice cube trays, then stored in plastic recloseable bags for later use. Peel can also be wrapped and frozen for later use.

To zest an orange, use the fine edge of a cheese grater, ensuring you don't grate the white pith underneath. Or use a zester to remove the zest, then finely chop. Zesters are inexpensive and widely available at specialty kitchen shops.

1	medium onion, finely chopped	1
1 1/2 lbs	carrots, cut into 1-inch (2.5 cm) chunks (about 5 cups [1.25 L])	750 g
3 cups	chicken stock	750 mL
	Juice of 1 orange	
	Zest of 1 orange	
1/2 cup	whipping (35%) cream	125 mL
	Salt and black pepper to taste	

1. In slow cooker, combine onion, carrots, stock and orange juice. Cover and cook on **Low** for 10 to 12 hours or on **High** for 4 to 6 hours, until carrots are fork tender.

2. Strain vegetables, reserving stock. In a blender or food processor, purée vegetables until smooth. Transfer back to slow cooker and add zest and cream. Season to taste with salt and pepper. Reheat on **High** for 15 minutes.

No-Fuss Chicken or Turkey Stock

Makes 6 cups (1.5 L)

Nothing could be easier than this homemade stock. Put all the ingredients in the slow cooker and let it simmer all day or overnight. Then make the tastiest soup ever!

TIP

You can use this stock for a variety of soups and recipes in this book, but it works especially well with ROYAL CHICKEN SOUP (see recipe, page 55) or BOXING DAY TURKEY SOUP (see recipe, page 41).

You can also make stock using the leftover carcass from a cooked chicken or turkey. Remove all the meat first and refrigerate or freeze until ready to use. If you don't have time to make the stock right away, don't fret. Just keep the carcass frozen for up to 4 months.

3 lbs	chicken leg quarters (separated) *or* 2 turkey thighs, skin on	1.5 kg
1	onion, quartered	1
1	carrot	1
1	celery stalk (with leaves)	1
8 to 10	whole peppercorns	8 to 10
1	bay leaf	1
2 tsp	salt	10 mL
	Water (about 6 to 8 cups [1.5 to 2 L])	

1. Place chicken pieces, onion, carrot, celery stalk, peppercorns, bay leaf and salt in slow cooker; cover with water. Cover and cook on **Low** for 8 to 10 hours or on **High** for 4 to 6 hours.
2. Strain broth through cheesecloth-lined sieve into a large bowl, pressing vegetables to extract as much liquid as possible. Discard vegetables, reserving chicken.
3. Cover and refrigerate broth overnight; remove congealed fat from surface. Remove meat from bones and discard bones and skin. Refrigerate stock and chicken for up to 3 days or freeze for up to 4 months.

I'd-Swear-it-was-Pizza Soup

Serves 4 to 6

Your kids will love this soup, because it tastes like really good pizza. But I've found that its simple and delicious flavors are equally popular with adults.

The croutons in the bottom of each serving bowl are my substitute for a crunchy pizza crust.

TIP

If your kids dislike chunks in their food (as mine do), purée the tomatoes before adding them to the slow cooker.

VARIATION

You can substitute your favorite pizza meat topping for the pepperoni in this soup. Try cooked sweet or hot Italian sausage, ham or cooked ground beef.

☾ NIGHT BEFORE

This soup can be assembled 12 to 24 hours in advance of cooking (but without adding pepperoni, green pepper and mozzarella cheese). Follow preparation directions and refrigerate overnight in slow cooker stoneware. The next day, place stoneware in slow cooker and cook as directed.

1	onion, chopped	1
1 cup	sliced mushrooms (about 5 or 6 medium)	250 mL
1	can (28 oz [796 mL]) Italian-style stewed tomatoes, with juice	1
1 cup	beef stock	250 mL
1 cup	thinly sliced pepperoni	250 mL
1	medium green pepper, chopped	1
1/2 cup	croutons	125 mL
1 cup	grated mozzarella cheese	250 mL

1. In slow cooker, combine onion, mushrooms, tomatoes and stock; stir to mix well.
2. Cover and cook on **Low** for 5 to 6 hours or on **High** for 3 to 4 hours. Add pepperoni and green pepper during last 30 minutes of cooking.
3. Divide croutons equally between individual bowls. Spoon soup over croutons and top each with grated mozzarella cheese.

Curried Cream of Chicken Soup

Serves 4 to 6

This hearty meal-in-a-bowl can be made ahead up to the point of adding the peas and cream. (In fact, allowing it to sit in the fridge for 24 hours gives the flavors even more opportunity to develop.) Reheat on **High** for 2 to 3 hours or **Low** for 4 to 6 hours. Add cream and peas 15 minutes before serving.

You can also freeze the purée. Prepare soup purée as directed and freeze for up to 1 month. Diced cooked chicken can be frozen for up to 1 month, as well. Reheat previously thawed purée in the slow cooker on **High** for 2 to 3 hours or on **Low** for 4 to 6 hours. Add cream, reserved thawed chicken and peas. Heat on **Low** for 15 to 20 minutes.

1	large onion, chopped	1
2	carrots, chopped	2
1 1/2 tbsp	curry powder	20 mL
5 cups	chicken stock	1.25 L
1/4 cup	parsley	50 mL
1	chicken (about 2 to 3 lbs [1 to 1.5 kg]), quartered	1
1/2 cup	long grain rice	125 mL
1 cup	half-and-half (10%) cream *or* light (5%) cream	250 mL
1 cup	frozen peas	250 mL
	Salt and black pepper to taste	

1. In slow cooker, combine onion, carrots, curry powder, stock, parsley, chicken pieces and rice; stir to mix well. Cover and cook on **Low** for 8 to 10 hours or on **High** for 4 to 6 hours.

2. With a slotted spoon, gently remove chicken pieces from stock. Set aside to cool slightly. Remove meat from bones; dice chicken and reserve. Discard bones and skin.

3. Transfer vegetables and stock to a blender or food processor. In batches, purée mixture until smooth; return to slow cooker. Add cream, reserved chicken and peas. Adjust seasoning, adding more curry powder if desired. Heat on **Low** for 15 to 20 minutes. Season to taste with salt and pepper.

Spicy Vegetable-Lentil Soup

Serves 4 to 6

Don't worry about any over-whelming spiciness here. This surprisingly sweet tasting soup will warm you to your toes.

TIP

TIP

Serve with toasted whole-wheat pitas and a dollop of plain yogurt.

Red lentils are available in cans, but the dried variety cook up so fast that they're the better (and cheaper) choice. It is important to pick over lentils to remove any sticks or broken pieces, then rinse and drain before using. If the holes in your strainer are too large, line it with a paper towel before rinsing.

NIGHT BEFORE

This soup can be assembled 12 to 24 hours in advance. Follow preparation directions and refrigerate overnight in slow cooker stoneware. The next day, place stoneware in slow cooker and cook as directed.

4	medium carrots, diced	4
2	stalks celery, diced	2
1	medium large onion, diced	1
1	medium Granny Smith apple, peeled, cored and diced	1
1 tbsp	grated peeled ginger root	15 mL
1	large clove garlic, minced	1
1 tbsp	curry powder	15 mL
3/4 tsp	ground cumin *or* cumin seeds	4 mL
4 cups	chicken stock	1 L
1/2 cup	dried red lentils, rinsed (see Tip, at left)	125 mL
	Plain low-fat yogurt	

1. In slow cooker, combine carrots, celery, onion, apple, ginger root, garlic, curry, cumin, stock and lentils; stir to mix well.
2. Cover and cook on **Low** for 8 to 10 hours or on **High** for 4 to 6 hours, until thick and bubbling.
3. Transfer mixture to a blender or food processor. In batches, purée until smooth. Return to slow cooker to keep warm. Ladle soup into individual bowls and top each with a dollop of yogurt.

Harvest Corn Chowder with Bacon and Cheddar

Serves 8 to 10

The slow cooker isn't just for wintertime fare. I love to make this soup when the harvest of fresh corn appears in late July and August.

TIP

To use fresh sweet corn in this recipe, remove the husks and stand cobs on end. Use a sharp knife and cut kernels off cobs.

Serve with a hearty multigrain bread or bagels and glasses of ice-cold lemonade.

For a meatless version, omit bacon and add all ingredients to slow cooker. Cook as directed.

MAKE AHEAD

This soup can be made up to the point of thickening. Refrigerate for 3 days or freeze up to 3 months. To reheat, thaw first, place soup in slow cooker with 1/2 cup (125 mL) water, cover and reheat on **High** for 2 to 3 hours or on **Low** for 4 to 6 hours. Continue with Step 3 as directed.

4	slices bacon, chopped	4
2	medium onions, chopped	2
2	stalks celery, chopped	2
2	medium potatoes, chopped	2
4 cups	corn kernels, fresh or frozen	1 L
4 cups	chicken stock	1 L
1	bay leaf	1
1 tsp	salt	5 mL
1/2 tsp	black pepper	2 mL
2 tbsp	butter *or* margarine	25 mL
2 tbsp	all-purpose flour	25 mL
1	can (13 oz [385 mL]) evaporated milk *or* 1 1/2 cups (375 mL) whipping (35%) cream	1
1 cup	grated Cheddar cheese	250 mL
	Cheddar cheese	
	Chopped fresh parsley	

1. In a large nonstick skillet over medium heat, cook bacon, onions and celery for 5 minutes or until onions are translucent. With a slotted spoon, transfer mixture to slow cooker.

2. Add potatoes, corn, stock, bay leaf, salt and pepper to slow cooker; stir to combine. Cover and cook on **Low** for 8 to 10 hours or on **High** for 4 to 6 hours, until vegetables are tender and soup is bubbling. Remove bay leaf and discard.

3. In a saucepan over medium-high heat, melt butter. Add flour and stir to make a smooth paste. Slowly add milk, whisking constantly to combine. Bring mixture to a boil, whisking constantly until thickened. Remove from heat and stir in cheese until completely melted. Gradually stir milk sauce mixture into slow cooker. Cover and cook on **High** for 20 to 30 minutes. Serve garnished with additional Cheddar cheese and chopped fresh parsley.

Rich Vegetable Broth with Meatballs

Serves 4 to 6

This is a perfect soup to serve guests after a day of winter activities.

TIP

If you need a few more servings, this soup can be extended by adding pasta such as fusilli or rotini.

Serve with warm foccacia bread or a thick Italian loaf to soak up the sauce.

I like to make an extra batch of the meatballs used in this soup. They're great to have on hand to use in quick appetizers or pasta sauces. They freeze well and keep in the freezer for up to 3 months.

PREHEAT OVEN TO 350° F (180° C)
BAKING SHEET, FOIL-LINED

1 lb	lean ground beef	500 g
1/2 cup	fine dry breadcrumbs	125 mL
1 tbsp	chopped fresh parsley	15 mL
1 tsp	salt	5 mL
1/4 tsp	black pepper	1 mL
1	egg, lightly beaten	1
2	medium onions, finely chopped	2
2	carrots, finely chopped	2
1	stalk celery, finely chopped	1
1	can (19 oz [540 mL]) Italian-style tomatoes, with juice	1
2 cups	beef stock	500 mL
1/4 tsp	dried oregano	1 mL
1/4 tsp	dried basil	1 mL
1	bay leaf	1
	Parmesan cheese	

1. In a large bowl, combine ground beef, breadcrumbs, parsley, salt, pepper and egg; mix thoroughly. With your hands, shape into 1/2-inch (1 cm) meatballs. Transfer to prepared baking sheet and bake in preheated oven for 20 minutes. Set aside to cool.

2. In slow cooker, combine onions, carrots, celery, tomatoes, stock, oregano, basil, and bay leaf. Add cooked meatballs.

3. Cover and cook on **Low** for 8 to 10 hours on **High** for 4 to 6 hours, until hot and bubbling. Remove bay leaf and discard. Spoon into individual bowls and garnish with Parmesan cheese.

New England-Style Clam Chowder

Serves 6 to 8

On a recent trip to Boston, I tried the clam chowder at every restaurant I visited. Each claimed to be "the best" – and they *were* very good. I think this one rates right up there too!

TIP

Remember not to add the clams until the end; they will get tough if cooked too long.

For a meatless version, omit bacon. Add onion, celery and green pepper directly to the slow cooker. Continue cooking as directed.

To avoid lumps in soups and stews, place liquid and flour in a jar with a tight-fitting lid. Shake well and pour into hot stock mixture.

6	strips bacon, finely chopped	6
1	onion, finely chopped	1
3	stalks celery, finely chopped	3
2	cans (each 5 oz [142 g]) whole baby clams	2
1 cup	water	250 mL
3 cups	diced peeled potatoes	750 mL
1 tsp	Worcestershire sauce	5 mL
1/2 tsp	salt	2 mL
1/4 tsp	black pepper	1 mL
1	bay leaf	1
1/4 cup	all-purpose flour	50 mL
2 cups	light (5%) cream *or* half-and-half (10%) cream *or* 1 can (13 oz [385 mL]) evaporated milk	250 mL
Half	green pepper, finely chopped	Half

1. In a large nonstick skillet, sauté bacon, onion and celery for 5 minutes or until vegetables are softened and onion is translucent. With a slotted spoon, transfer mixture to slow cooker.
2. Drain clam liquid into slow cooker; set aside whole clams. Add water, potatoes, Worcestershire sauce, salt, pepper and bay leaf.
3. Cover and cook on **High** for 3 to 4 hours or on **Low** for 6 to 10 hours, until potatoes are tender and soup is bubbling. Remove bay leaf and discard.
4. In a bowl combine flour and 1/4 cup (50 mL) cream; mix well to dissolve lumps. Add to slow cooker along with reserved whole clams, green pepper and remaining cream. Cover and cook on **High** for 25 to 30 minutes or until thickened.

Potato-Leek Soup with Stilton

Serves 4 to 6

This is a classic French soup with an English twist – Stilton cheese has been one of our family favorites for years!

TIP

Serve with lots of crumbled Stilton cheese and a loaf of French bread.

Blue cheese or Roquefort cheese can be substituted for Stilton, but the flavor won't be the same.

Leeks have thick white bodies and broad green leaves that resemble an overgrown green onion. They have a uniquely mild, sweet flavor, and I find them an essential ingredient for many soups.

Leeks must be cleaned carefully, since they contain a lot of sand. Remove most of the green part and cut the white part into halves lengthwise. Rinse thoroughly under cold running water and drain in a colander.

MAKE AHEAD

This soup can be prepared up to the point before adding cream. It can be refrigerated up to 2 days or frozen for up to 3 months. To reheat, add 1 cup (250 mL) water and heat until piping hot.

2 tbsp	butter *or* margarine	25 mL
3	leeks (white parts only), trimmed, well rinsed and sliced	3
1	medium onion, chopped	1
4	medium potatoes, peeled and chopped	4
6 cups	chicken stock	1.5 L
1 tsp	salt	5 mL
1/2 tsp	black pepper	2 mL
Pinch	ground nutmeg	Pinch
1 cup	whipping (35%) cream	250 mL
	Crumbled Stilton cheese	
	Salt and pepper to taste	

1. In a large pot, heat butter over medium-high heat. Add leeks and onion; cover, reduce heat to medium-low and cook for 10 minutes or until tender. Transfer to a slow cooker.

2. Add potatoes, stock, salt, pepper and nutmeg. Cover and cook on **Low** for 8 to 10 hours or on **High** for 4 to 6 hours, until vegetables are tender.

3. Transfer soup to a blender or food processor. In batches, purée soup until smooth. Season to taste with salt and pepper. Return soup to slow cooker; stir in cream. Cover and cook on **High** 15 to 20 minutes or until heated through. Crumble cheese into bottom of individual serving bowls and ladle in soup. If desired, sprinkle with additional Stilton. Season to taste with salt and pepper.

Roasted Red Pepper and Tomato Soup

Serves 4 to 6

When I walk through our local farmer's market in August and September, I am overcome with an incredible urge to make as many dishes as I can with the bountiful display of lush, ripe tomatoes and red peppers. This is one of my favorites.

TIP

In season, red bell peppers are very inexpensive, so I broil or grill extra and keep them in the freezer to have on hand during the winter months.

If you make this soup in the winter, use vine-ripened tomatoes for best flavor. Add an extra tablespoon (15 mL) of tomato paste after the mixture is puréed.

To ripen tomatoes, place in a paper bag and leave on the counter at room temperature. Never store tomatoes in the refrigerator; it dulls their delicate flavor.

PREHEAT BROILER
COOKIE SHEET

4	large red bell peppers	4
5	large tomatoes, peeled, seeded and chopped *or* 1 can (28 oz [796 mL]) Italian-style plum tomatoes, with juice	5
1	medium onion, finely chopped	1
1	stalk celery, finely chopped	1
2	fresh basil leaves (or 1/2 tsp [2 mL] dried)	2
2 cups	chicken stock	500 mL
1 tbsp	tomato paste	15 mL
2 tsp	granulated sugar	10 mL
	Juice of half a lemon	
	Salt and black pepper to taste	
	Fresh basil	
	Whipping (35%) cream (optional)	

1. Cut peppers in half and remove seeds. Place cut-side down on cookie sheet. Broil or grill until skins are blackened and puffed. Remove from oven and place in a paper bag to steam. When cooled, peel off and discard skins; cut pepper into chunks.

2. Transfer peppers to slow cooker. Add tomatoes, onion, celery, basil, stock and tomato paste. Cover and cook on **Low** for 4 to 6 hours or on **High** for 2 to 3 hours. Transfer to a blender or food processor and process until smooth.

3. Return mixture to slow cooker. Stir in sugar, lemon juice and salt and pepper to taste. Serve hot or refrigerate and serve cold. Garnish with snips of fresh basil. For a richer soup, drizzle 1 to 2 tbsp (15 to 25 mL) whipping cream into soup bowl before serving.

Royal Chicken Soup

Serves 6 to 8

My friend and colleague Pat Morris runs the kitchens at the Royal Agricultural Winter Fair held in Toronto every November. With so many fresh root vegetables on hand, the home economists always whip up a batch of this soup for the media. Its wonderful flavor keeps them coming back for more. Now you can enjoy it too!

TIP

If time won't allow you to make homemade chicken stock, use the next best thing – canned. Avoid using bouillon mix or cubes, since these can be extremely salty and don't give the same rich taste.

6 cups	No-Fuss Chicken Stock (see recipe, page 46) or 3 cans (each 10 oz [284 mL]) chicken broth, diluted with an equal amount of water	1.5 L
3	leeks (white parts only), chopped	3
4	carrots, sliced	4
2	stalks celery, finely chopped	2
2	parsnips, diced	2
2 cups	diced cooked chicken	500 mL
1/4 cup	chopped fresh parsley	50 mL
1/2 tsp	paprika	2 mL
2 cups	cooked egg noodles	500 mL
	Salt and black pepper to taste	

1. In slow cooker, combine stock, leeks, carrots, celery, parsnips, chicken, parsley and paprika.
2. Cover and cook on **Low** for 8 to 10 hours or on **High** for 4 to 6 hours, until vegetables are tender and soup is bubbling.
3. In a large pot of boiling salted water, cook noodles according to package directions. Drain well. Add to slow cooker; stir to combine. Season to taste with salt and pepper.

Squash and Apple Soup

Serves 4 to 6

Of all the vegetables I serve my children, squash is their least favorite. However, they love this soup and always ask for more.

TIP

This recipe can easily be doubled and it freezes well.

For a decorative touch on the Thanksgiving table, scoop out seeds and stringy bits of a small pumpkin. Pour hot soup into pumpkin and serve.

VARIATION

Any buttery squash, such as Hubbard or Acorn, can be used in this recipe. You can also substitute 1 can (28 oz [796 mL]) canned pumpkin purée (not pie filling) for the squash.

☾ NIGHT BEFORE

This soup can be assembled 12 to 24 hours in advance of cooking (but without adding the cheese). Prepare ingredients as directed in slow cooker stoneware and refrigerate overnight. The next day place stoneware in slow cooker and cook as directed.

1	butternut squash (about 3 lbs [1.5 kg]), peeled and cut into 1-inch (2.5 cm) cubes	1
2	apples, peeled, cored and chopped	2
1	medium onion, chopped	1
3 cups	chicken stock	750 mL
1 cup	apple juice	250 mL
1/2 tsp	dried marjoram	2 mL
1/2 tsp	dried thyme	2 mL
1/2 tsp	salt	2 mL
1/2 tsp	black pepper	2 mL
1/2 cup	grated Swiss cheese	125 mL

1. In slow cooker, combine squash, apples, onion, stock, juice, marjoram, thyme, salt and pepper.
2. Cover and cook on **Low** for 8 to 10 hours or on **High** for 4 to 6 hours, until squash is tender.
3. In a colander strain soup, reserving liquid. Transfer mixture to a blender or food processor. Add 1 cup (250 mL) reserved liquid and process until smooth.
4. Return soup to the slow cooker along with remaining stock. Season to taste with additional salt and pepper. Spoon into serving bowls and top each with grated Swiss cheese.

That's-a-Lotta-Beans Soup

Serves 4 to 6

1 lb	mild Italian sausage, casings removed	500 g
1	jar (28 oz [796 mL]) 7-bean mix, with liquid	1
1	can (28 oz [796 mL]) tomatoes, diced, with juice	1
4	carrots, peeled and diced	4
2 cups	chicken stock	500 mL
1 tsp	dried Italian seasoning	5 mL
2	zucchini, diced	2
	Grated Parmesan cheese	
	Salt and black pepper to taste	

TIP

I can't think of anything better than coming in from the cold and being met by the aroma of this soup simmering in the slow cooker and a loaf of hearty bread baking in the bread machine.

If you can't find a jar of 7-bean mixture, look for a dried version of this mixture in the bulk food section of the supermarket. Before using, soak the beans: cover 2 cups (500 mL) dry bean mixture with 8 cups (2 L) water and simmer on stovetop for 1 hour or until beans are tender. Drain and add to slow cooker as directed.

For a meatless version, omit the sausage. Add 1 tbsp (15 mL) chili powder and 1 tbsp (15 mL) chopped garlic, 1/2 tsp (2 mL) red pepper flakes and increase Italian seasoning to 1 tbsp (15 mL).

☾ NIGHT BEFORE

This soup can be assembled 12 to 24 hours in advance of cooking (but without adding zucchini and cheese). Prepare ingredients as directed in slow cooker stoneware and refrigerate overnight. The next day, place stoneware in slow cooker and cook as directed.

1. In a skillet over medium-high heat, brown sausage, stirring to break up meat. With a slotted spoon, transfer to slow cooker.

2. Add bean mix with liquid, tomatoes with juice, carrots, stock and Italian seasoning. Cover and cook on **Low** for 8 to 10 hours or on **High** for 4 to 6 hours, until vegetables are tender. Add zucchini and cook for another 15 to 20 minutes.

3. Spoon into individual bowls and top with grated Parmesan cheese. Season to taste with salt and pepper.

French Canadian Split Pea Soup

Serves 6 to 8

Making a pot of hearty pea soup to enjoy after outdoor activities is a wonderful winter tradition.

TIP

A thick, crusty bun and warm tea or glass of crisp white wine is all that's needed for a tasty meal.

Split peas will be very tough unless they are soaked before making the soup. They can either be left to stand in water overnight or boiled for 2 minutes and left to stand for 1 hour.

🌙 NIGHT BEFORE

It is best to start making this soup 12 to 24 hours in advance – in fact all the ingredients can be assembled in the slow cooker stoneware and refrigerated overnight. The next day, before heading outside for a day of winter activities, place stoneware in slow cooker, and cook as directed. A simmering pot will await you upon your return.

1 lb	yellow split peas	500 g
8 oz	smoked pork hock (skin removed)	250 g
3	medium carrots, diced	3
1	large potato, peeled and diced	1
1	stalk celery, finely chopped	1
1	bay leaf	1
1/4 tsp	thyme	1 mL
1/4 tsp	basil	1 mL
1/4 tsp	oregano	1 mL
	Salt and black pepper to taste	

1. Place peas in a bowl and add enough cold water to cover; soak peas for at least 12 hours (Alternatively, place peas in a pot, cover with water, bring to a boil, remove from heat and let stand for 1 hour.) Rinse well and place in slow cooker. Add 7 cups (1.75 L) water, smoked pork hock, carrots, potato, celery, bay leaf, thyme, basil and oregano.

2. Cover and cook on **Low** for 10 to 12 hours or on **High** for 6 to 8 hours, until soup is thick and bubbling.

3. With a slotted spoon, gently remove pork hock from soup. Remove meat from bone, cut into chunks and return to pot. Remove bay leaf and discard. Serve immediately and season to taste with salt and pepper.

Chilies & Beans

DRIED BEANS

Cooking dried beans from scratch takes a little extra time, but it's very economical and, in many people's opinion, gives a better-tasting result than using canned beans. When using dried beans, remember that the beans will more than double in size after cooking. One pound (500g) dried beans yields approximately 4 to 5 cups (1 to 1.25 L) cooked beans. Also bear in mind that beans must be completely cooked before combining with sugar or acidic foods such as molasses or tomatoes. (Sugar and acid tend to prevent beans from softening.)

Preparing Dried Beans
Transforming the hard, dried legume into a tender, edible bean requires four steps: cleaning, soaking, rinsing and cooking. Soaking the beans helps to replace the water that has been lost in the drying process. It also speeds up the cooking time. Cooking times for beans (see chart below) depend on the type of slow cooker used, as well as the variety, age and quality of the beans, altitude and whether hard or soft water is used in cooking. The best way to test for doneness is to taste them. Cooked beans are free of any raw, starchy taste, are fork tender, and easy to squash between your fingers.

Begin by picking the beans over to remove any that are broken or cracked, then place them in a colander or sieve and rinse well under cold running water. In a pot of boiling water (enough to cover beans), simmer on the stovetop for 10 minutes; drain and rinse well. Transfer beans to a slow cooker and cover with 6 cups (1.5 L) fresh water per pound (500 g) beans. Cover and cook on **Low** for about 12 hours. Discard water unless otherwise stated. Beans are now recipe-ready. (Hint: Let the beans do the initial cooking in the slow cooker while you are sleeping and they will be recipe-ready in the morning.)

BEAN TYPE	SUGGESTED COOKING TIME
Red Kidney Beans	10 to 12 hours on **Low**
Light Red Kidney Beans	10 to 12 hours on **Low**
White Kidney Beans	10 to 12 hours on **Low**
White Pea or Navy Beans	10 to 12 hours on **Low**
Black Beans	8 to 10 hours on **Low**
Romano/Cranberry Beans	8 to 10 hours on **Low**
Chickpeas/Garbanzo Beans	10 to 12 hours on **Low**

Storing Cooked Beans
Cooked beans store well in the refrigerator in resealable plastic bags or covered containers for up to 5 days. Cooked beans can also be kept in the freezer for up to 6 months. For convenient, easy meals, it's a good idea to pack them in measured amounts, such as 1 cup (250 mL) or 2 cups (500 mL) – amounts usually called for in recipes.

CANNED BEANS

For convenience, the same variety of canned beans may be substituted for cooked, dried beans in any of the recipes in this book. One 19-oz (540 mL) can of any bean variety can be substituted for 2 cups of cooked beans. Canned beans are already cooked and are recipe-ready. Before adding to any recipe, rinse well under cold running water to remove brine. Canned beans should be stored in a cool, dry place and, for best flavor and texture, should be used within a year of purchase.

Anthony's Awesome Chili Con Carne

Serves 6 to 8

My friend Anthony Scian gave me his "secret" recipe for this very flavorful chili. It's cocoa powder – something Mexican cooks have used for centuries to make their mole sauces.

TIP

For those who like their chili a little spicier, add more cayenne pepper.

Small quantities of leftover chili should never go to waste. Try spooning this chili over hot baked potatoes. Garnish with grated Cheddar cheese.

◑ NIGHT BEFORE

This chili can be assembled 12 hours in advance of cooking (but without adding the green pepper). Follow preparation directions and refrigerate overnight in slow cooker stoneware. The next day, place stoneware in slow cooker and continue cooking as directed.

2 lbs	lean ground beef	1 kg
2	large cloves garlic, minced	2
2	stalks celery, finely chopped	2
2	large onions, finely chopped	2
2 tbsp	chili powder	25 mL
1/2 tsp	dried oregano	2 mL
1/4 tsp	cayenne pepper	1 mL
1	can (28 oz [796 mL]) tomatoes, diced, with juice	1
1	can (19 oz [540 mL]) red kidney beans, drained and rinsed *or* 2 cups (500 mL) soaked, cooked and drained beans	1
2 tbsp	cocoa powder	25 mL
1 tbsp	brown sugar	15 mL
3 or 4	whole cloves	3 or 4
1 tsp	white vinegar	5 mL
1/2 tsp	black pepper	2 mL
1	medium green pepper, finely chopped	1
	Salt and black pepper to taste	

1. In a large nonstick skillet over medium heat, combine ground beef, garlic, celery and onions. Cook until vegetables are tender and meat is no longer pink. Add chili powder, oregano and cayenne; cook 1 minute longer. With a slotted spoon, transfer mixture to a slow cooker.

2. Add tomatoes (with juice), kidney beans, cocoa, sugar, cloves, vinegar and pepper; stir to combine. Cover and cook on **Low** for 6 to 8 hours or on **High** for 3 to 4 hours, until hot and bubbling. Add green pepper and stir to combine. Cover and cook 20 to 25 minutes longer. Season to taste with salt and pepper.

Chicken and Black Bean Chili in Tortilla Bowls

Serves 6

CHILI

1 tbsp	vegetable oil	15 mL
2 lbs	boneless skinless chicken breast, cut into 1/2-inch (1 cm) cubes	1 kg
1	medium onion, finely chopped	1
2	cloves garlic, minced	2
1	can (19 oz [540 mL]) tomatoes, chopped, with juice	1
1	can (12 oz [341 mL]) corn kernels *or* 1 1/2 cups (375 mL) frozen corn	1
1	can (19 oz [540 mL]) black beans, rinsed and drained *or* 2 cups (500 mL) soaked, cooked and drained black beans	1
2 cups	mild or hot salsa	500 mL
1 tbsp	chili powder	15 mL
1/2 tsp	salt	2 mL

TORTILLA BOWLS

6	large flour tortilla shells	6
	Lettuce leaves, washed	
1	tomato, diced	1
2	jalapeño peppers, chopped	2

1. In a large nonstick skillet, heat oil over medium heat. Add chicken and cook, stirring frequently, until chicken is no longer pink. With a slotted spoon, transfer to a slow cooker.
2. Add onion, garlic, tomatoes (with juice), corn, black beans, salsa, chili powder and salt; stir to combine. Cover and cook on **Low** for 4 to 6 hours or on **High** for 2 to 3 hours, until hot and bubbling.

3. Tortilla Bowls: Mold a piece of foil around the inside of a 6-cup (1.5 L) mixing bowl. Gently press one tortilla into foil bowl. Remove foil and tortilla together and place on a large baking sheet. Tortilla will have folds.) Repeat with more foil and tortillas to make 2 more tortilla bowls. Bake in preheated oven for 15 to 20 minutes or until tortillas are crisp and golden. Place tortillas on a wire rack to cool. Repeat bowl-making procedure using same foil to make another 3 tortilla bowls for a total of 6 bowls.

4. To assemble, place one tortilla bowl on each plate. Line each bowl with lettuce leaves. Spoon in chili and garnish with tomato and jalapeño peppers.

Party Pleas'n Chili

Serves 8 to 10

TIP

This dish goes down beautifully with a bottle of full-bodied red wine.

The best cut of beef to buy for this chili is an economical round steak or stewing beef. Don't use an expensive cut like flank steak, it will just fall apart from the long slow-cooking process.

Red pepper flakes. This fiery flavor booster can be found in the spice section of the supermarket. Leave on the table for a great season-ing alternative to salt and pepper.

☾ NIGHT BEFORE

This chili can be assembled 12 hours in advance of cook-ing (with the exception of red and green pepper). Follow preparation directions and refrigerate overnight in slow cooker stoneware. The next day, place stoneware in slow cooker and continue cooking as directed.

1 tbsp	vegetable oil	15 mL
1 lb	round steak, cut into 1-inch (2.5 cm) cubes	500 g
1 lb	hot Italian sausage, casings removed	500 g
2	large onions, finely chopped	2
1	can (28 oz [796 mL]) tomatoes, chopped, with juice	1
1	can (19 oz [540 mL]) red kidney beans, drained and rinsed or 2 cups (500 mL) soaked, cooked and drained kidney beans	1
1	can (19 oz [540 mL]) black beans, drained and rinsed or 2 cups (500 mL) soaked, cooked and drained black beans	1
1	can (5.5 oz [156 mL]) tomato paste	1
1/2 cup	red wine	125 mL
4	cloves garlic, minced	4
2 tbsp	chili powder	25 mL
1 tbsp	dried oregano	15 mL
1 tbsp	Dijon mustard	15 mL
1 tsp	black pepper	5 mL
1/2 tsp	red pepper flakes (optional)	2 mL
1/2 tsp	salt	2 mL
1	red bell pepper, finely chopped	1
1	green pepper, finely chopped	1
	Chopped red onions	
	Monterey Jack cheese, shredded	
	Tortilla chips	

Recipe continues next page...

STRATFORD'S SWEET CHILI (PAGE 70) ➤

OVERLEAF: SIMPLE SALMON PIE WITH CREAMY DILL SAUCE (PAGE 82) ➤

1. In a large nonstick skillet, heat oil over medium-high heat. Add steak cubes and cook for 7 to 8 minutes or until brown on all sides. Using a slotted spoon, transfer to slow cooker, reserving juices. Return pan with juices to heat; add sausage and onions and cook, breaking up meat with a spoon (adding more oil if necessary). When meat is no longer pink inside, drain and transfer to slow cooker.

2. Add tomatoes (with juice), kidney beans, black beans, tomato paste, red wine, garlic, chili powder, oregano, Dijon mustard, pepper, red pepper flakes (if using) and salt; stir to combine. Cover and cook on **Low** for 8 to 10 hours or on **High** for 4 to 6 hours, until hot and bubbling. Add red pepper and green pepper; cover and cook on **High** for another 20 to 25 minutes.

3. Serve with chopped red onions, shredded Monterey Jack cheese and tortilla chips.

◄ VEGETABLE PASTITSIO (PAGE 80)

Chunky Beef Chili

Serves 4 to 6

1 tbsp	vegetable oil	15 mL
2 lbs	stewing beef, cut into 1/2-inch (1 cm) cubes	1 kg
2 tbsp	chili powder	25 mL
1 tsp	ground cumin	5 mL
1 tsp	dried oregano	5 mL
3/4 tsp	salt	4 mL
2	medium onions, chopped	2
2	carrots, chopped	2
2	stalks celery, chopped	2
1	can (19 oz [540 mL]) tomatoes, diced, with juice	1
1	can (19 oz [540 mL]) chickpeas, drained and rinsed *or* 2 cups (500 mL) soaked, cooked and drained chickpeas	1
1 cup	beef stock	250 mL
Half	can (5.5 oz [156 mL]) tomato paste	Half
1	red bell pepper, chopped	1

1. In a large nonstick skillet, heat oil over medium heat. Add beef cubes and cook for 7 to 8 minutes or until browned on all sides. Add chili powder, cumin, oregano and salt; cook 1 minute longer. With a slotted spoon, transfer meat to slow cooker.

2. Add onions, carrots, celery, tomatoes (with juice), chickpeas, stock and tomato paste; stir to combine. Cover and cook on **Low** for 8 to 10 hours or on **High** for 4 to 6 hours. Add red pepper; stir to combine. Cover and cook on **High** for another 20 to 25 minutes.

Football Sunday Chili

Serves 4 to 6

Everyone needs a good chili for football season, whether it's a tailgate party or in the comfort of your own home. This is also a perfect potluck tote! It's a mildly hot chili with a slightly sweet flavor.

If you have a large (6-quart) slow cooker, this recipe can easily be doubled. I love to serve this with hot garlic bread or buttered toast.

There are over 100 varieties of hot peppers and some are definitely hotter than others. The general rule – the smaller the chili, the bigger the heat.

When handling hot peppers, make sure you keep your hands away from your eyes. Better yet, wear rubber gloves and wash hands and utensils afterwards.

◑ NIGHT BEFORE

This chili can be assembled 12 hours in advance of cooking (but without adding the green pepper). Follow preparation directions and refrigerate overnight in slow cooker stoneware. The next day, place stoneware in slow cooker and continue cooking as directed.

2 lbs	lean ground beef	1 kg
2	large onions, chopped	2
2	hot red chili peppers, seeded and finely chopped	2
2 tbsp	chili powder	25 mL
1 tsp	ground ginger	5 mL
1 tsp	cinnamon	5 mL
1/2 tsp	ground allspice	2 mL
1/2 tsp	ground nutmeg	2 mL
1	can (28 oz [796 mL]) tomatoes, diced, with juice	1
1	can (10 oz [284 mL]) condensed tomato soup	1
2	cans (19 oz [540 mL]) red kidney beans, drained and rinsed *or* 2 cups (500 mL) soaked, cooked and drained kidney beans	2
1/2 cup	cider vinegar	125 mL
1/4 cup	packed brown sugar	50 mL
2	green peppers, finely chopped	2

1. In a large nonstick skillet over medium-high heat, cook ground beef, onions and hot peppers until ground beef is fully cooked and no longer pink. Add chili powder, ginger, cinnamon, allspice and nutmeg; cook 1 minute longer. With a slotted spoon, transfer seasoned meat to a slow cooker.

2. Add tomatoes (with juice), tomato soup, kidney beans, vinegar and brown sugar; stir to combine. Cover and cook on **Low** for 8 to 10 hours or on **High** for 4 to 6 hours, until hot and bubbling. Add green pepper, stirring to combine. Cover and cook another 20 to 25 minutes.

Saucy-Blonde Chili

Serves 4 to 6

Made with lean ground pork, chicken or turkey, this saucy dish is lighter in color than the average chili.

Canned green chilies are found in the Mexican food section of the supermarket. They are sold chopped or whole.

Make a second meal out of MOLASSES BAKED BEANS (see recipe, page 76) by using them in this recipe instead of canned beans. The results will be completely different, but taste great! If desired, serve over hot cooked rice or noodles.

This chili can be assembled 12 hours in advance of cooking. Follow preparation directions and refrigerate overnight in slow cooker stoneware. The next day, place stoneware in slow cooker and continue cooking as directed.

1 tbsp	vegetable oil	15 mL
1 1/2 lbs	lean ground pork, chicken or turkey	750 g
1	medium onion, finely chopped	1
2	cloves garlic, minced	2
1 tbsp	chili powder	15 mL
1/2 tsp	ground cumin	2 mL
2	cans (each 14 oz [398 mL]) beans in tomato sauce	2
1 cup	chicken stock	250 mL
1	can (4.5 oz [127 mL]) chopped green chilies, with liquid	1
	Salt and black pepper to taste	

1. In a nonstick skillet, heat oil over medium-high heat. Add pork, onion and garlic, cooking until meat is no longer pink and onion is translucent. Add chili powder and cumin; cook 1 minute longer. With a slotted spoon, transfer mixture to slow cooker.

2. Add beans, stock and chilies (with liquid); stir to combine. Cover and cook on **Low** for 6 to 8 hours or on **High** for 3 to 4 hours, until hot and bubbling. Season to taste with salt and pepper.

Spicy Turkey Chili

Serves 4 to 6

My children love chili served with tortilla chips. Look for yellow or blue ones – either way, everyone will enjoy scooping and eating.

1 tbsp	vegetable oil	15 mL
2 lbs	ground turkey	1 kg
1	onion, finely chopped	1
1 tsp	red pepper flakes	5 mL
1 tsp	ground coriander	5 mL
1 tsp	ground cumin	5 mL
1/2 tsp	salt	2 mL
1/4 tsp	black pepper	1 mL
2	cans (19 oz [540 mL]) navy or white pea beans, rinsed and drained *or* 2 cups (500 mL) soaked, cooked and drained beans	2
2 cups	chicken stock	500 mL
1	can (12 oz [341 mL]) corn kernels *or* 2 cups (500 mL) frozen corn	1
1	can (4.5 oz [127 mL]) chopped mild green chilies, drained	1
1 cup	chopped fresh cilantro	250 ml

1. In a nonstick skillet, heat oil over medium heat. Add ground turkey, onion, red pepper flakes, coriander and cumin; cook, breaking up meat with a spoon, for 5 to 7 minutes or until no longer pink. With a slotted spoon, transfer seasoned turkey to slow cooker.

2. Add salt, pepper, 1 can of beans, stock, corn and chilies. In a bowl with a potato masher or in a food processor, mash or purée remaining can of beans. Add to slow cooker and stir to combine.

3. Cover and cook on **Low** for 6 to 10 hours or on **High** for 3 to 4 hours, until chili is hot and bubbling. Add cilantro, cover and cook on **High** for another 15 to 20 minutes.

Stratford's Sweet Chili

Serves 6 to 8

My childhood friend Joy Stratford has been a vegetarian for many years. Not only is she a busy mom and great soccer player, she is also a fantastic cook! This is one of her favorite recipes.

TIP

If you find this chili too sweet, reduce the honey by 2 tbsp (25 mL).

Substitute 1 cup (250 mL) frozen corn for canned corn.

Beans are an excellent source of fiber and protein, and give this chili a hearty, filling consistency that satisfies even a die-hard meat eater. Don't be afraid to add an additional can of beans to this recipe. Several varieties of shapes and colors add interest and texture.

🌙 NIGHT BEFORE

This chili can be assembled 12 hours in advance of cooking. Follow preparation directions and refrigerate overnight in slow cooker stoneware. The next day, place stoneware in slow cooker and continue cooking as directed.

1	can (19 oz [540 mL]) chickpeas, drained and rinsed *or* 2 cups (500 mL) soaked, cooked and drained chickpeas	1
1	can (19 oz [540 mL]) red kidney beans or black beans, drained and rinsed *or* 2 cups (500 mL) soaked, cooked and drained beans	1
1	can (28 oz [796 mL]) tomatoes with herbs and spices, chopped	1
1	can (10 oz [284 mL]) corn kernels, drained	1
2	carrots, peeled and diced	2
2	large cloves garlic, minced	2
1	red onion, finely chopped	1
1 cup	ketchup	250 mL
1/4 cup	liquid honey	50 mL
3 tbsp	chili powder	45 mL
1/2 tsp	cayenne pepper	2 mL
1	green pepper, diced	1
1	red bell pepper, diced	1
1	yellow pepper, diced	1
	Sour cream	
	Cheddar cheese, grated	

1. In slow cooker, combine chickpeas, kidney beans, tomatoes, corn, carrots, garlic and red onion. In a bowl combine ketchup, honey, chili powder and cayenne; mix well and pour into slow cooker. Stir mixture to combine.

2. Cover and cook on **Low** for 8 to 10 hours or on **High** for 4 to 6 hours, until hot and bubbling. Add green pepper, red pepper, yellow pepper and cook on **High** for an additional 20 to 25 minutes. Serve in bowls with a dollop of sour cream and grated Cheddar cheese.

Hearty Vegetarian Chili

Serves 6

This dish is a spicy blend of squash, carrots, black beans and more – you'll never miss the meat!

TIP

You can substitute two large sweet potatoes (peeled and chopped) for the squash.

Fresh cilantro, also known as coriander or Chinese parsley, has a very distinctive smell and flavor that suits many chilies, as well as oriental and Indian dishes. To maximize its fairly short refrigerator shelf-life, wash the leaves well, spin-dry and wrap in paper towels. Store in a plastic bag in the fridge. If the cilantro has roots attached, leave them on – it helps keep the leaves fresh.

Canned green chilies are found in the Mexican food section of the supermarket. They are sold whole or chopped.

☾ NIGHT BEFORE

This chili can be assembled 12 hours in advance of cooking. Follow preparation directions and refrigerate overnight in slow cooker stoneware. The next day, place stoneware in slow cooker and continue cooking as directed.

1	medium-sized butternut squash, peeled and cut into 3/4-inch (2 cm) cubes	1
2	medium carrots, diced	2
1	medium onion, finely chopped	1
1	can (28 oz [796 mL]) tomatoes, diced, with juice	1
2	cans (each 19 oz [540 mL]) black beans, rinsed and drained *or* 4 cups (1 L) soaked, cooked and drained black beans	2
1	can (4.5 oz [127 mL]) chopped green chilies, with liquid	1
1 cup	vegetable or chicken stock	250 mL
3 tbsp	chili powder	45 mL
1/2 tsp	salt	2 mL
1/4 cup	chopped fresh cilantro (see Tip, at left)	50 mL
	Sour cream	
	Fresh cilantro, chopped	

1. In slow cooker, combine squash, carrots, onion, tomatoes (with juice), black beans, chilies (with liquid), stock, chili powder and salt; stir to mix well.

2. Cover and cook on **Low** for 6 to 8 hours or on **High** for 3 to 4 hours, until hot and bubbling. Add cilantro; cover and cook on **High** 15 to 20 minutes longer. Spoon into serving bowls and top with a dollop of sour cream and additional chopped fresh cilantro.

Winter Chicken and Corn Chili

Serves 4 to 6

TIP

For convenience, roasted red peppers are available in jars or can be found fresh in the deli section of some super-markets. To make your own, preheat broiler and cut red peppers in half, removing pith and seeds. Place cut-side down on cookie sheet. Broil until all skin turns black. Place in paper bag and close up. Allow peppers to sweat for approximately 30 minutes. Peel off skins and chop as needed.

MAKE AHEAD

Peppers can be broiled or grilled, peeled, then frozen for later use. They will keep up to 3 months in the freezer.

1 tbsp	vegetable oil	15 mL
2 lbs	ground chicken	1 kg
3 or 4	green onions, finely chopped	3 or 4
2 tsp	chili powder	10 mL
1/2 tsp	dried oregano	2 mL
Pinch	cayenne pepper	Pinch
2	roasted red bell peppers, diced	2
2 tbsp	pickled jalapeño peppers, finely chopped	25 mL
3	cloves garlic, minced	3
1	bay leaf	1
1	can (19 oz [540 mL]) navy beans or white kidney beans, rinsed and drained *or* 2 cups [500 mL] soaked, cooked and drained beans	1
1 1/2 cups	frozen corn kernels	375 mL
1 1/2 cups	chicken stock	375 mL
1/2 cup	chopped fresh cilantro	125 mL
2 tbsp	lime juice	25 mL
1 tbsp	granulated sugar	15 mL
1/2 tsp	salt	2 mL
	Sour cream	

1. In a nonstick skillet, heat oil over medium-high heat. Add chicken and green onions; cook, breaking up meat with a spoon, 4 to 6 minutes or until chicken is no longer pink. Add chili powder, oregano and cayenne; cook 1 minute longer. With a slotted spoon, transfer mixture to slow cooker.
2. Add red peppers, jalapeño peppers, garlic, bay leaf, beans, corn, and stock; stir to combine.
3. Cover and cook on **Low** for 6 to 8 hours or on **High** for 3 to 4 hours. Discard bay leaf. Stir in cilantro, lime juice, sugar and salt. Cover and cook on **High** 10 minutes longer or until heated through. Ladle into bowls and garnish with a dollop of sour cream.

Best Ever Baked Beans

Serves 12 to 15

I like to take this dish to our annual skating party and sleigh ride. When there are a lot of people, it's the perfect pot-to-pack.

Serve these beans with garlic bread and a green salad.

This dish can be assembled in the slow cooker the day before. Refrigerate until ready to cook.

8 oz	bacon	250 g
1 lb	lean ground beef	500 g
2	onions, sliced and separated into rings	2
4 cups	MOLASSES BAKED BEANS (see recipe, page 76) *or* 2 cans (each 14 oz [398 mL]) beans in tomato sauce	1 L
1	can (19 oz [540 mL]) red kidney beans, rinsed and drained *or* 2 cups (500 mL) soaked, cooked and drained beans	1
1	can (19 oz [540 mL]) chickpeas, rinsed and drained *or* 2 cups (500 mL) soaked, cooked and drained chickpeas	1
2 cups	ketchup	500 mL
1/4 cup	granulated sugar	50 mL
1/4 cup	brown sugar	50 mL
3 tbsp	white vinegar	45 mL
1 tbsp	Dijon mustard	15 mL

1. In a large nonstick skillet over medium-high heat, cook bacon for 5 minutes or until slightly cooked but not crisp. Remove from skillet and place on paper-towel lined plate. Cool and coarsely chop. Drain excess fat from skillet. Add ground beef and onions to skillet; cook, breaking up meat, for 7 to 8 minutes or until browned and onions are translucent. With a slotted spoon, transfer meat mixture to slow cooker.

2. Add baked beans, kidney beans, chickpeas, ketchup, granulated sugar, brown sugar, vinegar and mustard; stir to combine.

3. Cover and cook on **Low** for 7 to 9 hours or on **High** for 3 to 4 hours, until bubbling.

Black Bean Moussaka

Serves 6 to 8

In this vegetarian version of Greek-style lasagna, noodles and meat are replaced with hearty eggplant and black beans. It's a wonderful make-ahead for a buffet supper at the chalet.

TIP

Tired of opening a whole can of tomato paste when all you need is a small amount? Look for the squeeze tubes of tomato paste sold in most supermarkets.

If not salted first, eggplant develops a bitter flavor in the slow cooker. Sprinkle cut eggplant with salt. Place in a colander, cover with a plate and weight down with heavy cans. Allow eggplant to drain for 1 hour, then rinse under cold water to remove salt and pat dry with paper towels.

☾ NIGHT BEFORE

This chili can be assembled 12 hours in advance of cooking. Follow preparation directions and refrigerate overnight in slow cooker stoneware. The next day, place stoneware in slow cooker and continue cooking as directed.

1	large eggplant, peeled and cut into 2-inch (5 cm) cubes	1
	Salt	
2 tbsp	olive oil	25 mL
1	large onion, finely chopped	1
1	can (19 oz [540 mL]) tomatoes, chopped, with juice	1
1/4 cup	red wine	50 mL
2 tbsp	tomato paste	25 mL
1 tsp	dried oregano	5 mL
1/4 tsp	cinnamon	1 mL
2	cans (each 19 oz [540 mL]) black beans, rinsed and drained *or* 4 cups (1 L) soaked, cooked and drained black beans	1

TOPPING

1 cup	milk	250 mL
2	eggs	2
2 tbsp	butter *or* margarine	25 mL
2 tbsp	all-purpose flour	25 mL
1/2 tsp	salt	2 mL
1/4 tsp	black pepper	1 mL
1/4 tsp	ground nutmeg	1 mL
1/2 cup	grated Mozzarella cheese	125 mL

1. Place chopped eggplant in a colander and sprinkle with salt; cover with a plate. Let stand for 1 hour or until the eggplant releases its juices. Rinse well under cold running water to remove salt, then drain. Squeeze out any excess moisture and pat dry with paper towels.

2. In a large skillet, heat half the oil over medium-high heat. Add eggplant and sauté for 10 minutes or until lightly browned. Remove to a plate and set aside. Return skillet to heat and add remaining 1 tbsp (15 mL) oil. Add onion and sauté for 5 minutes or until tender. Add tomatoes (with juice), red wine, tomato paste, oregano and cinnamon. Bring mixture to a boil, reduce heat and simmer for 5 minutes. Stir in black beans and set aside.

3. Topping: In a 2-cup (500 mL) measure, combine milk and eggs. Mix well and set aside. In a saucepan heat butter over medium-low heat. Add flour, stirring to combine. Increase heat to medium and gradually whisk in egg mixture, whisking constantly until slightly thickened. Add salt, pepper and nutmeg.

4. To assemble: Into prepared slow cooker, place half the sautéed eggplant. Spoon tomato-bean mixture over eggplant. Add remaining eggplant and cover with topping. Sprinkle with mozzarella cheese.

5. Cover and cook on **Low** for 8 to 10 hours or on **High** for 4 to 6 hours, until bubbling. Let stand for 5 minutes before serving.

Molasses Baked Beans

Nothing is as heartwarming as a pot of these comfy baked beans. The marriage of ketchup, molasses and sugar is what makes them so flavorful. Not only are they extremely tasty, they are also very nutritious and a good source of protein and fiber.

TIP

White pea beans, also known as navy beans or *alubias chicas*, are the type of cooked bean you will find in "pork and beans" or, as will be called for in many recipes, "beans in tomato sauce." The term "navy bean" was adopted during the Second World War, when this dish was regularly fed to the troops. It is important to soak the beans first to replace the water lost in drying.

VARIATION

Salsa Beans: Substitute bottled salsa for ketchup and add 1 tsp (5 mL) ground cumin and 1 tsp (5 mL) dried oregano. Increase black pepper to 1 tsp (5 mL).

4 cups	water	1 L
1 lb	dry white pea or navy beans	500 g
6 cups	cold water	1.5 L
1	onion, chopped	1
1	can (5.5 oz [156 mL]) tomato paste	1
3/4 cup	ketchup	175 mL
3/4 cup	molasses	175 mL
2	cloves garlic, minced	2
1/3 cup	packed brown sugar	75 mL
2 tsp	dry mustard	10 mL
1/2 tsp	salt	2 mL
1/4 tsp	black pepper	1 mL

1. In a large pot over medium-high heat, bring water to a boil. Add beans and simmer for 10 minutes. Drain and rinse.

2. Transfer beans to slow cooker and add about 6 cups (1.5 L) cold water or enough to completely cover beans. Cover and cook on **Low** 10 to 12 hours or until fork tender. Drain, reserving 2 cups (500 mL) cooking liquid.

3. In a bowl combine onion, tomato paste, ketchup, molasses, garlic, sugar, mustard, salt and pepper; stir to mix well. Add to slow cooker with beans and reserved liquid. Cover and cook on **Low** for 4 to 6 hours or on **High** for 2 to 3 hours, until beans are hot and bubbling.

Pasta & Pot Luck
Favorites

Fia's Favorite Pasta Sauce

Makes about 12 cups (3 L)

My friend Fia grew up in an Italian household in Toronto. She has fond memories of coming home from school where a pot of pasta sauce was always simmering on the stove. She passed her secret sauce along to me and I've adapted it for the slow cooker. Now my children always ask for Fiasauce.

TIP

Freeze sauce in 2-cup (500 mL) batches and thaw for quick use in other recipes. Try it with VEGETABLE PASTITSIO (see recipe, page 80), CHEESY TORTELLINI BAKE (see recipe, page 87) or SPICY WHITE BEAN AND SAUSAGE RAGOUT (see recipe, page 128).

☾ NIGHT BEFORE

This sauce can be completely assembled 12 to 24 hours in advance. Place all ingredients in slow cooker stoneware and refrigerate overnight. The next day, place stoneware in slow cooker and cook as directed.

4	cans (each 28 oz [796 mL]) Italian plum-style tomatoes, coarsely chopped, with juice	4
1 cup	red wine	250 mL
1/2 cup	olive oil	125 mL
1/4 cup	freshly chopped parsley (or 2 tbsp [25 mL] dried)	50 mL
4	cloves garlic, minced	4
2 tsp	salt	10 mL
1 tsp	red pepper flakes	5 mL
1 tsp	dried oregano	5 mL
8	fresh basil leaves (or 1 tsp [5 mL] dried)	8
1 tsp	black pepper	5 mL
	Hot cooked pasta	
	Parmesan cheese	

1. In slow cooker, combine tomatoes (with juice), wine, olive oil, parsley, garlic, salt, red pepper flakes, oregano, basil and pepper.
2. Cover and cook on **Low** for 8 to 10 hours or **High** for 4 to 6 hours, until sauce is hot and bubbling.
3. Serve over hot cooked pasta and sprinkle with Parmesan cheese.

Basic Spaghetti Sauce Italiano

Makes 6 cups

This is my favorite recipe for spaghetti sauce. It makes enough for a couple of meals. If you have a small amount left over, spoon it over a split baked potato and add a dollop of sour cream for a satisfying quick meal.

Slow cooking with ground meat. It is always best to brown ground meat before adding it to the slow cooker. This ensures the meat is completely cooked and reaches the recommended cooked temperature of 150° F (65° C). If you have a good nonstick skillet, you will not need to add any extra fat (from cooking oil) unless you are browning ground turkey or chicken, which is generally very lean.

MENU SUGGESTION

BASIC SPAGHETTI SAUCE ITALIANO
   WITH PASTA
Caesar Salad
Italian Bread
Cappuccino Ice Cream and
   Biscotti

1 tbsp	vegetable oil	15 mL
2 lbs	lean ground beef, turkey or chicken	1 kg
4	cloves garlic, minced	4
2	onions, finely chopped	2
2	stalks celery, finely chopped	2
1 tbsp	dried oregano	15 mL
1/2 tsp	dried thyme	2 mL
1/2 tsp	dried basil	2 mL
1	can (28 oz [796 mL]) tomatoes, diced, with juice	1
1	can (5.5 oz [156 mL]) tomato paste	1
1	bay leaf	1
1 tbsp	brown sugar	15 mL
1/2 tsp	salt	2 mL
1/2 tsp	hot pepper flakes (optional)	2 mL
	Salt and black pepper	
	Hot cooked spaghetti	

1. In a large skillet, heat oil over medium-high heat. Add beef and cook until browned, breaking up meat with a spoon. As it cooks, add garlic, onions, celery, oregano, thyme and basil. Cook for 2 to 3 minutes or until vegetables are tender. With a slotted spoon, transfer seasoned meat mixture to slow cooker.

2. Add tomatoes (with juice), tomato paste, bay leaf, sugar, salt and hot pepper flakes, if using. Stir to combine.

3. Cover and cook on **Low** for 8 to 10 hours or on **High** for 4 to 6 hours, until hot and bubbling. Remove bay leaf and discard. Season sauce to taste with salt and pepper. Serve over hot cooked spaghetti or other pasta.

Vegetable Pastitsio

Serves 6 to 8

A savory vegetable mixture is layered over spinach and creamy pasta in this delicious variation of lasagna.

TIP

You can use 1 cup (250 mL) FIA'S FAVORITE PASTA SAUCE (see recipe, page 78) in place of canned tomato sauce.

◑ NIGHT BEFORE

This dish takes quite a bit of preparation time, but fortunately it can be completely assembled up to 24 hours in advance. Follow preparation directions and refrigerate overnight in the slow cooker stoneware. The next day, place stoneware in slow cooker and continue cooking as directed. It's perfect for a buffet supper or potluck reunion.

MENU SUGGESTION

Vegetable Pastitsio
Tossed Green Salad
Italian Bread
Strawberry Tarts

PASTA CUSTARD LAYER

3 cups	dried penne or any small pasta	750 mL
1/4 cup	butter *or* margarine	50 mL
1/4 cup	all-purpose flour	50 mL
1	can (13 oz [385 mL]) evaporated milk	1
1/2 tsp	ground nutmeg	2 mL
1/2 tsp	salt	2 mL
1/4 tsp	black pepper	1 mL
2	eggs, lightly beaten	2
1 cup	small-curd cottage cheese	250 mL
1 cup	grated mozzarella cheese	250 mL

VEGETABLE LAYER

1 tbsp	vegetable oil	15 mL
1	medium onion, finely chopped	1
2	cloves garlic, minced	2
1	small zucchini, finely chopped (about 1 cup [250 mL])	1
1	carrot, peeled and grated	1
1 cup	frozen corn kernels	250 mL
1	small can (7.5 oz [213 mL]) tomato sauce	1
1/2 tsp	dried oregano	2 mL
1/4 tsp	cinnamon	1 mL
1/4 tsp	black pepper	1 mL
1	pkg (11 oz [300 g]) frozen chopped spinach, thawed	1
1/4 cup	Parmesan cheese	50 mL

1. In a pot of boiling, salted water, cook pasta according to package directions. Drain and rinse well with cold water. Set aside.

2. In a heavy saucepan, heat butter over medium heat. Add flour and cook, stirring constantly to prevent browning, for 2 minutes. Gradually add milk, whisking constantly until smooth. Cook for 5 minutes or until thickened. Stir in nutmeg, salt and pepper.

3. In a large bowl, combine eggs with about 1/2 cup (125 mL) sauce, mixing well. Add remaining sauce, cottage cheese, mozzarella cheese and reserved pasta. Set aside.

4. In a large skillet, heat oil over medium heat. Add onion, garlic, zucchini and carrot; cook for 5 minutes or until vegetables are softened. Add corn, tomato sauce, oregano, cinnamon and pepper. Bring to a boil, reduce heat and simmer for 5 minutes.

5. Spoon pasta mixture into prepared slow cooker insert. Spread spinach over pasta and spoon vegetable mixture over spinach. Sprinkle with Parmesan cheese. Cover and cook on **Low** for 6 to 9 hours or on **High** for 3 to 4 hours, until mixture is bubbling. Let stand for 10 minutes before serving.

Simple Salmon Pie with Creamy Dill Sauce

Serves 4 to 6

My mother, Evelyn Pye, spent countless hours with my sisters and me at the dance studio. When we got home, one of her specialties (and one of our favorites) was salmon loaf. This slow-cooker version is easy to make and can quickly be put together. And of course, you must serve it with steaming green peas – the *only* way, according to Ev!

TIP

For an economical pie, use 1 can (7.5 oz [213 g]) sockeye salmon and 1 can (7.5 oz [213 g]) of the less expensive pink salmon.

For a larger pie, double all ingredients, using 4 cans salmon.

This pie makes a wonderful complete meal when served with boiled new potatoes, green peas and asparagus, and lemon custard for dessert.

NIGHT BEFORE

This dish can be completely assembled up to 12 hours in advance of cooking. Follow preparation directions and refrigerate overnight in the slow cooker stoneware. The next day, place stoneware in slow cooker and continue cooking as directed.

SLOW COOKER STONEWARE INSERT, LIGHTLY GREASED

2	cans (each 7.5 oz [213 g]) red sockeye salmon, drained, skin removed	2
1/4 cup	finely crushed saltine crackers	50 mL
1	small onion, finely chopped	1
1	egg, lightly beaten	1
2 tbsp	milk or light (5%) cream	25 mL
1 tbsp	lemon juice	15 mL
1 tbsp	chopped fresh parsley (or 1 tsp [5 mL] dried)	15 mL
1 tbsp	chopped fresh dill (or 1 tsp [5 mL] dried)	15 mL
1/2 tsp	black pepper	2 mL

CREAMY DILL SAUCE

1 tbsp	butter *or* margarine	15 mL
1 tbsp	all-purpose flour	15 mL
1/2 tsp	salt	2 mL
1/4 tsp	black pepper	1 mL
1 cup	milk	250 mL
2 tbsp	chopped fresh dill (or 2 tsp [10 mL] dried)	25 mL

1. Fold a 2-foot (60 cm) piece of aluminum foil in half lengthwise twice, and place on bottom and up the sides of prepared slow cooker stoneware. In a bowl combine salmon, crackers, onion, egg, milk, lemon juice, parsley, dill and pepper. Using a fork or wooden spoon, gently mix until evenly combined. Press evenly into foil-lined slow cooker. Tuck ends of foil under lid. (For a large oval-style slow cooker, salmon mixture can be shaped into a loaf and set on foil handles.)

2. Cover and cook on **Low** for 4 to 6 hours or on **High** for 2 to 2 1/2 hours. To remove, turn off heat and let pie stand for 5 minutes. Gently run a knife around outside edge of pie and lift out with foil handles. Set on plate and place lifter between loaf and foil; lift loaf from foil, remove foil and set loaf onto serving plate.

3. Creamy Dill Sauce: In a saucepan melt butter over medium heat. Add flour, salt and pepper; cook, stirring, for 1 minute. Gradually whisk in milk; cook, stirring constantly, for 5 minutes or until boiling and thickened. Stir in dill. Serve over salmon.

Kid's Favorite
Tuna Noodle Casserole

Serves 4 to 6

TIP

Serve this casserole with a
crisp green salad.

Evaporated milk holds up
extremely well in slow cooking and will not curdle. In this
dish, you can use the low-fat
2% partly skimmed type.
Don't confuse this milk with
"condensed milk" – the sweet
sugary one used in desserts
and candy.

MAKE AHEAD

This dish can be completely
assembled (but without
adding topping mixture) up
to 12 hours in advance of
cooking. Follow preparation
directions and refrigerate
overnight in slow cooker
stoneware.

SLOW COOKER STONEWARE INSERT, LIGHTLY GREASED

1 tbsp	butter *or* margarine	15 mL
8 oz	mushrooms, sliced or finely chopped	250 g
1	onion, finely chopped	1
2 tbsp	all-purpose flour	25 mL
1 cup	chicken stock	250 mL
1	can (13 oz [385 mL]) evaporated milk	1
4 oz	light cream cheese, cut into 1/2-inch (1 cm) cubes	125 g
1	can (6.5 oz [184 g]) solid white tuna, drained and flaked	1
1 cup	frozen peas	250 mL
	Salt and black pepper to taste	
8 oz	penne or rotini pasta, uncooked	250 g

TOPPING

1/2 cup	crushed corn flake-type cereal	125 mL
1 tbsp	melted butter	15 mL
1 cup	grated Cheddar cheese	250 mL

1. In a large nonstick skillet, heat butter over medium heat. Add mushrooms and onion; cook for 5 minutes or until mushrooms have released their juices and onion is softened.

2. Add flour, stirring to blend. Pour in stock and evaporated milk. Bring mixture to a boil, stirring constantly until slightly thickened. Stir in cream cheese until melted. Add tuna and peas, stirring to combine. Remove from heat. Season to taste with salt and pepper.

3. Meanwhile, cook pasta in a pot of boiling, salted water according to package directions or until tender but firm. Drain and toss with tuna mixture. Transfer mixture to prepared slow cooker.

Kid's Favorite Tuna Noodle Casserole

Tossed Green Salad

Blueberry Crisp

4. Topping: In a bowl toss together cereal and melted butter. Add Cheddar cheese, stirring to combine. Sprinkle over noodles in slow cooker. Cover and cook on **Low** for 4 to 6 hours or on **High** for 1 1/2 to 2 hours, until bubbling and heated through.

Morrocan Vegetable Hotpot

Serves 4 to 6

This hearty Moroccan-inspired stew combines squash and chickpeas, lightly scented with fragrant cinnamon. It is best served over hot, fluffy couscous.

TIP

For a meaty version, stir in 2 cups (500 mL) chopped cooked chicken when adding parsley. Cook 15 to 20 minutes longer or until heated through.

Couscous is another name for semolina, the milled center of durum wheat. It is traditionally served with North African dishes – particularly those from Morocco, Algeria and Tunisia – and it takes less time to prepare than rice. Simply stir 1 cup (250 mL) couscous with 1 1/4 cups (300 mL) boiling water, 1 tbsp (15 mL) butter and 1/4 tsp (1 mL) salt. Cover and let stand for 5 minutes, then fluff with a fork.

☾ NIGHT BEFORE

This dish can be completely assembled the night before. Follow preparation directions and refrigerate overnight in the slow cooker stoneware. The next day, place stoneware in slow cooker and continue cooking as directed.

2	carrots, sliced	2
1	medium butternut squash, peeled and cut into 1-inch (2.5 cm) cubes	1
1	medium onion, chopped	1
1	can (19 oz [540 mL]) chickpeas, rinsed and drained	1
1	can (19 oz [540 mL]) tomatoes, diced, with juice	1
1 cup	vegetable or chicken stock	250 mL
1/2 cup	chopped pitted prunes	125 mL
1 tsp	cinnamon	5 mL
1/2 tsp	red pepper flakes	2 mL
2 tbsp	chopped fresh parsley or cilantro	25 mL
	Salt and black pepper to taste	
	Hot couscous (see note, at left)	

1. In slow cooker, combine carrots, squash, onion, chickpeas, tomatoes (with juice), stock, prunes, cinnamon and red pepper flakes; stir to mix well.

2. Cover and cook on **Low** for 6 to 8 hours or on **High** for 3 to 4 hours, until all vegetables are tender.

3. Before serving, stir parsley into stew and season to taste with salt and pepper. Serve over hot cooked couscous.

Cheesy Tortellini Bake

Serves 6 to 8

This recipe is perfect family fare or as a potluck take-a-long.

TIP

For a great meal, serve with bruschetta, a tossed green salad, and cappuccino ice cream.

Roasted red pepper sauce is widely available in many grocery stores. Look for it in the refrigerated deli department near the fresh pasta. If you can't find any, substitute 3 cups [750 mL] of your favorite canned or bottled pasta sauce or FIA'S FAVORITE PASTA SAUCE (see recipe, page 78) for the roasted red pepper sauce and tomato sauce.

☾ NIGHT BEFORE

Assemble and refrigerate overnight in slow cooker stoneware. The next day, place stoneware in liner and cook as directed.

2 lbs	cheese-filled tortellini	1 kg
1	container (about 14.6 oz [415 g]) roasted red pepper sauce	1
1	small can (7.5 oz [213 mL]) tomato sauce	1
1	can (19 oz [540 mL]) pasta-style stewed tomatoes, with juice	1
2 cups	grated Cheddar cheese	500 mL
2 tbsp	grated Parmesan cheese	25 mL
	Chopped fresh parsley	

1. In a pot of boiling water, cook pasta according to package directions; drain. In a bowl combine red pepper sauce and tomato sauce; mix well

2. Spoon one-third red pepper sauce mixture in bottom of prepared slow cooker insert. Layer with half the cooked noodles, all the tomatoes (with juice), one-third red pepper sauce mixture and half the Cheddar cheese. Cover with remaining noodles, remaining one-third red pepper sauce mixture and remaining Cheddar cheese. Sprinkle with grated Parmesan cheese and chopped parsley.

3. Cover and cook on **Low** for 4 to 6 hours or on **High** for 2 to 3 hours, until bubbling.

Mexican Weekend Brunch Bake

Serves 6 to 8

This is an ideal brunch or light supper idea – sausage and eggs with a Mexican twist. All the work is done the night before. Invite company after church and the food is ready. *Olé!*

TIP

Mild green chilies are found in the Mexican foods section of the supermarket. They are sold whole or chopped.

Look for corn tortillas in the deli department of the supermarket or where flour tortillas are sold. If you have difficulty finding them, substitute tortilla chips. Don't use flour tortillas, since they will become soggy.

WEEKEND BRUNCH

*MEXICAN WEEKEND BRUNCH BAKE
Fresh Fruit Kabobs
Coffee Cake or Cinnamon Rolls
Coffee/Tea*

2 lbs	hot or mild Italian sausage, casings removed	1 kg
2	cans (each 4.5 oz [128 g]) chopped green chilies	2
4	corn tortillas, cut into 1-inch (2.5 cm) strips	4
2 cups	grated Monterey Jack or Mexican-style cheese combination	500 mL
1/2 cup	milk	125 mL
8	eggs	8
1/2 tsp	ground cumin	2 mL
	Paprika	
1	tomato, thinly sliced	1
	Salsa	
	Sour cream	

1. In a large nonstick skillet, cook sausage over medium-high heat, breaking up with a spoon. Drain well.

2. In prepared slow cooker insert, layer half the green chilies, half the tortilla strips, half the sausage and then half the cheese. Repeat layers.

3. In a bowl, beat together milk, eggs and cumin. Pour over sausage mixture. Sprinkle with paprika. Cover and refrigerate overnight.

4. The next day, set insert in slow cooker. Top with tomato slices. Cover and cook on **Low** for 7 to 9 hours or on **High** for 3 to 4 hours. Skim off any accumulated fat. Serve topped with salsa and sour cream.

Lentil Curry with Squash and Cashews

Serves 6

For the vegetarian in the family or for adding to your array of meatless entrées, try this Middle-Eastern inspired dish.

A bowlful of this curry makes a hearty meal. Serve with warm pita bread.

For a meaty version, add chopped leftover chicken at the same time that you add the spinach.

While cooked green lentils are available in cans, the dried variety are fast and easy to cook. It is important to pick over lentils to remove any sticks or broken pieces, then rinse and drain before using.

2 tsp	vegetable oil	10 mL
1	medium onion, chopped	1
2	cloves garlic, minced	2
2 tbsp	all-purpose flour	25 mL
1 tbsp	curry powder	15 mL
1 tbsp	grated peeled ginger root (or 1 tsp [5 mL] ground ginger)	15 mL
1 tsp	ground cumin	5 mL
1 tsp	fennel seeds	5 mL
1 tsp	salt	5 mL
2 cups	vegetable or chicken stock	500 mL
1 cup	water *or* apple juice	250 mL
1 cup	dried green lentils, picked over and rinsed	250 mL
2 cups	peeled and chopped butternut squash	500 mL
1	large potato, chopped into 1-inch (2.5 cm) cubes	1
6 cups	fresh spinach leaves, washed and trimmed	1.5 L
1/2 cup	cashews (salted or unsalted)	125 mL

1. In a skillet heat oil over medium heat. Add onion and garlic and cook for 5 minutes or until softened and translucent. Stir in flour, curry, ginger root, cumin, fennel seeds and salt; mix well.

2. Stir in stock and water; bring to a boil, scraping up bits from bottom of skillet. Transfer mixture to slow cooker. Add lentils, squash and potato; stir to combine. Cover and cook on **Low** for 7 to 9 hours or on **High** for 3 to 4 hours.

3. Add spinach leaves; stir to combine. Cover and cook on **High** for another 15 minutes or until leaves have wilted. Spoon into individual bowls and sprinkle with cashews.

Remarkable Ratatouille

Serves 6 to 8

Here's my version of the classic Mediterranean vegetarian dish. It can be eaten as a main course with a crisp green salad or as a side dish with salmon or chicken. Any way you serve it, this ratatouille is excellent!

Eggplant can become bitter in the slow cooker if it is not salted first. Place chopped eggplant in a colander and sprinkle all cut surfaces with salt. Place a plate on top of eggplant and weight down with cans or other heavy objects. Allow to stand for about 1 hour. Rinse well and pat dry with paper towels. Small eggplants do not need salting as much as large, since their water content is not as high.

NIGHT BEFORE

This dish can be completely assembled up to 12 hours in advance of cooking. Follow preparation directions and refrigerate overnight in the slow cooker stoneware. The next day, place stoneware in slow cooker and continue cooking as directed.

3	small eggplants, cut into 1-inch (2.5 cm) cubes	3
1 tsp	salt	5 mL
3 tbsp	olive oil	45 mL
1 tbsp	butter *or* margarine	15 mL
1	large onion, thinly sliced and separated into rings	1
8 oz	mushrooms, sliced	250 g
1	can (28 oz [796 mL]) Italian-style tomatoes with herbs and spices, chopped, with juice	1
2 tbsp	grated Parmesan cheese	25 mL
1/4 cup	fine dry breadcrumbs	50 mL
1 tsp	Italian seasoning	5 mL
1 cup	grated mozzarella cheese	250 mL

1. In a large colander, toss eggplants with salt. Let stand for 1 hour or until cubes release their juices. Rinse well under cold running water to remove salt, then drain. Squeeze out any excess moisture and pat dry with paper towels. Set aside.

2. In a large nonstick skillet, heat 1 tbsp (15 mL) oil and the butter over medium heat. Add onion and mushrooms; sauté for 10 minutes or until softened. Remove with a slotted spoon to a plate and set aside.

3. Return skillet to heat and add remaining 2 tbsp (25 mL) olive oil. In batches, sauté drained eggplant cubes over medium heat for 10 minutes or until lightly browned.

4. In slow cooker, layer half the eggplant cubes. Top with onion mixture and half the tomatoes (with juice). Sprinkle with Parmesan cheese, then add remaining eggplant cubes and chopped tomatoes.

5. In a bowl combine breadcrumbs, Italian seasoning and mozzarella cheese; mix well and spoon over tomatoes and eggplant. Cover and cook on **Low** for 8 to 10 hours or on **High** for 4 to 6 hours, until bubbling.

Beef & Veal

Bargain Beef Stroganoff

Serves 4

This stroganoff is delicious and much more economical than the traditional version, which is usually made with filet of beef.

TIP

Serve with buttered wide egg noodles and a simple green vegetable such as steamed green beans or broccoli. To complete the meal, accompany it with a hearty red wine.

The most flavorful paprika comes from Hungary. It can range from mild to hot. Use whatever suits your taste.

VARIATION

Try this recipe with cubes of stewing veal instead of beef.

1/4 cup	all-purpose flour	50 mL
1 tsp	salt	5 mL
1/2 tsp	black pepper	2 mL
2 lbs	stewing beef, cut into 1-inch (2.5 cm) cubes	1 kg
1 tbsp	vegetable oil	15 mL
8 oz	small white button mushrooms, cleaned *or* large white mushrooms, quartered (about 2 cups [500 mL])	250 g
2	onions, thinly sliced	2
1 1/2 cups	beef stock	375 mL
3 tbsp	Worcestershire sauce	45 mL
3 tbsp	tomato paste	45 mL
2 tbsp	paprika	25 mL
1 1/2 tbsp	Dijon mustard	20 mL
1 cup	sour cream	250 mL
	Hot cooked egg noodles	

1. In a bowl or plastic bag, combine flour, salt and pepper. In batches, add beef to seasoned flour and toss to coat. In a large nonstick skillet, heat oil over medium-high heat. Add beef in batches and cook for 5 to 7 minutes or until browned on all sides. With a slotted spoon, transfer beef to slow cooker; add mushrooms and onions.

2. In a 2-cup (500 mL) measure, combine beef stock, Worcestershire sauce, tomato paste, paprika and mustard, mixing well. Pour into slow cooker.

3. Cover and cook on **Low** for 8 to 10 hours or on **High** for 4 to 6 hours, until bubbling. Stir in sour cream and serve over hot noodles.

Cheeseburger Sloppy Joes

Serves 4 to 6

This dish is a great choice for those nights when everyone is coming and going at different times, since you can leave it simmering in the slow cooker and people can help themselves.

TIP

Serve over toasted kaiser rolls or whole-wheat toast and add a tossed green salad for a delicious meal.

MENU SUGGESTION

Cheeseburger Sloppy Joes (on Kaisers)

Baked French Fries or Potato Wedges

Tossed Green Salad

Chocolate Cupcakes

2 lbs	lean ground beef or turkey	1 kg
1	medium onion, finely chopped	1
2	stalks celery, finely chopped	2
1	can (10 oz [284mL]) condensed tomato soup	1
1/4 cup	water	50 mL
2 tbsp	tomato paste	25 mL
1 tbsp	Worcestershire sauce	15 mL
2 tsp	dried Italian seasoning	10 mL
1 cup	1/2-inch (1 cm) cubes Cheddar cheese	250 mL
	Salt and black pepper	
4 to 6	kaiser buns, split and toasted	4 to 6

1. In a large nonstick skillet over medium-high heat, cook ground beef, breaking up with a spoon, until browned. With a slotted spoon, transfer meat to slow cooker.

2. Add onion to slow cooker, along with celery, tomato soup (undiluted), water, tomato paste, Worcestershire sauce and Italian seasoning, stirring to combine. Cover and cook on **Low** for 6 to 10 hours or on **High** for 3 to 4 hours.

3. Reduce heat to **Low**. Add cheese cubes. Cover and cook for another 10 to 15 minutes or until cheese melts. Season to taste with salt and pepper. Spoon mixture over half a kaiser bun and top with the other half.

Comforting Shredded Beef

Serves 4 to 6

Here's true comfort food at its best.

TIP

These succulent shreds of juicy roast beef can be served with mashed potatoes or used to make PHILLY BEEF WRAPS (see recipe page 104). Take comfort in the fact that if you have any leftovers, they won't be around for long!

Sirloin tip roast is a very lean cut of beef but ideal for shredding in this recipe. You can omit the brandy, if you wish, but it imparts a rich, dark color to the juice.

☾ NIGHT BEFORE

This dish can be completely assembled up to 12 hours in advance of cooking. Follow preparation directions and refrigerate overnight in the slow cooker stoneware. The next day, place stoneware in slow cooker and continue cooking as directed.

1	3- to 4-lb (1.5 to 2 kg) sirloin tip roast	1
	Salt and black pepper	
1 tbsp	vegetable oil	15 mL
1/4 cup	cognac or brandy (optional)	50 mL
2 cups	beef stock	500 mL
1 cup	red wine	250 mL
2	onions, sliced	2

1. Season roast to taste with salt and pepper. In a large skillet or Dutch oven, heat oil over medium-high heat. Add roast and cook, turning meat with a wooden spoon, for 10 minutes or until brown on all sides. Pour cognac over meat (if using) and flame with a match. Transfer meat to slow cooker.

2. Add stock to slow cooker, along with red wine and onions. Cover and cook on **Low** for 10 to 12 hours or on **High** for 6 to 8 hours, until meat is very tender. (If using a large [4- to 6-quart] slow cooker, meat may not be completely submerged in liquid; turn 2 or 3 times during cooking so exposed edges will not dry out.)

3. Remove meat from juice and let stand for 10 minutes. Using a fork, pull apart roast, following the natural grain of the meat. It should fall apart very easily. Serve with beef juice for dipping.

Creamy Veal and Mushroom Ragout

Serves 4 to 6

This wonderfully creamy, rich stew can be served to company, as well as family. Make sure you serve it over hot cooked egg noodles.

TIP

For convenience, look for pre-cut veal stewing cubes in the meat department of the supermarket. Or ask your butcher to cut the veal into cubes for you.

☾ NIGHT BEFORE

This dish can be completely assembled up to 12 hours in advance of cooking. Follow preparation directions and refrigerate overnight in the slow cooker stoneware. The next day, place stoneware in slow cooker and continue cooking as directed.

1/4 cup	all-purpose flour	50 mL
1 tsp	salt	5 mL
1/2 tsp	black pepper	2 mL
1/2 tsp	dried thyme	2 mL
1	3-lb (1.5 kg) boneless veal shoulder or leg, well trimmed and cubed	1
2 tbsp	vegetable oil	25 mL
8 oz	small button mushrooms *or* large white mushrooms, quartered	250 g
2	medium onions, chopped	2
2	cloves garlic, minced	2
1 cup	beef stock	250 mL
1/4 cup	dry sherry	50 mL
2 tbsp	tomato paste	25 mL
1/4 cup	whipping (35%) cream	50 mL
2 cups	frozen green peas	500 mL
	Salt and black pepper	
	Hot cooked egg noodles	

1. In a bowl or large plastic bag, combine flour, salt, pepper and thyme. In batches, add veal to flour mixture and toss to coat. Transfer to a plate. In a large skillet, heat half the oil over medium-high heat. Cook veal in batches, adding more oil as needed, for 7 to 8 minutes or until browned all over. Transfer veal to slow cooker, along with mushrooms, onions and garlic.

2. In a 2-cup (500 mL) glass measure, combine stock, sherry and tomato paste; mix well. Pour into slow cooker and stir to combine. Cover and cook on **Low** for 8 to 10 hours or on **High** for 4 to 6 hours, until meat is tender and sauce is bubbling.

3. Add cream and peas. Cover and cook on **High** 15 to 20 minutes longer or until heated through. Season to taste with salt and pepper. Serve over hot noodles.

Lumberjack Ribs

Serves 6

3 lbs	beef short ribs or braising ribs	1.5 kg
	Black pepper	
1	can (19 oz [540 mL]) Italian plum tomatoes, coarsely chopped	1
2 cups	carrots, finely chopped	500 mL
2	medium onions, thinly sliced	2
8	cloves garlic, minced	8
1/2 cup	chopped fresh parsley (or 1/4 cup [50 mL] dried)	125 mL
2 tbsp	tomato paste	25 mL
2 tbsp	red wine vinegar	25 mL
2 tbsp	brown sugar	25 mL
2 tsp	salt	10 mL
1/2 tsp	dry mustard	2 mL
1 tbsp	grated ginger root (or 1 tsp [5 mL] ground ginger)	15 mL
1	bottle (12 oz [341 mL]) beer	1
2 tbsp	prepared horseradish	25 mL

TIP

Beef braising ribs or short ribs are meaty bones about 4 to 6 inches (10 to 15 cm) long. Slow cooking makes them extremely flavorful and tender. But beware – these ribs require the hearty appetite of a hungry lumberjack! Horseradish is a must-have with these meaty morsels.

When purchasing short ribs, allow 2 servings for each 1 lb (500 g) of meat.

Broiling ribs allows them to brown and removes excess fat.

1. Position a broiler rack 6 inches (15 cm) from heat source. Place ribs on prepared baking sheet and sprinkle liberally with pepper. Broil in preheated oven, turning often, for 10 to 15 minutes or until browned on all sides. Transfer to a paper towel-lined plate to drain.

Recipe continues next page...

CHICKEN STEW WITH ROSEMARY DUMPLINGS (PAGE 148) ➤
OVERLEAF: ST. PATTY'S CORNED BEEF AND VEGGIES WITH MARMALADE-MUSTARD GLAZE (PAGE 106) ➤

2. In a bowl combine tomatoes, carrots, onions, garlic, parsley, tomato paste, vinegar, brown sugar, salt, dry mustard and ginger, mixing well to combine. Place half the vegetable mixture in slow cooker, lay ribs on top and spoon over remaining vegetable mixture. Pour beer over vegetables and meat.

3. Cover and cook on **Low** for 8 to 10 hours or on **High** for 4 to 6 hours. Transfer meat to a platter and keep warm.

4. Skim fat from the surface of cooking liquid and add horseradish; stir to combine. Transfer mixture, in batches, to a blender or food processor and process until smooth. Pour sauce over ribs and serve immediately.

≺ COCONUT BEEF CURRY (PAGE 112)

Easy Cabbage Roll Casserole

Serves 6 to 8

While everyone enjoys the great taste of cabbage rolls, they're a lot of work to make. This recipe is an easy alternative with the same great taste.

MENU SUGGESTION

Easy Cabbage Roll Casserole
Mashed Potatoes and Peas
Sliced Peaches and Yogurt

☾ NIGHT BEFORE

This dish can be completely assembled up to 12 hours in advance of cooking. Follow preparation directions and refrigerate overnight in the slow cooker stoneware. The next day, place stoneware in slow cooker and continue cooking as directed.

1 1/2 lbs	lean ground beef or turkey	750 g
2	medium onions, finely chopped	2
1	clove garlic, minced	1
1 tsp	salt	5 mL
1/4 tsp	black pepper	1 mL
1	small can (7.5 oz [221 mL]) tomato sauce	1
1 cup	water	250 mL
1	can (10 oz [284 mL]) condensed tomato soup	1
1/2 cup	long grain rice	125 mL
4 cups	shredded cabbage	1 L
1/3 cup	tomato juice *or* water	75 mL
	Sour cream	

1. In a large nonstick skillet over medium-high heat, combine ground beef, onions, garlic, salt and pepper; cook, breaking up meat with a spoon, until browned. Drain off any excess fat. Return to heat and add tomato sauce, water and half the can of tomato soup, mixing well. Add rice, stirring to combine.

2. Into prepared slow cooker, place half of meat mixture, then half of cabbage. Top with remaining meat mixture and remaining cabbage.

3. In a bowl combine remaining tomato soup with tomato juice, mixing well. Pour into slow cooker. Cover and cook on **Low** for 8 to 10 hours or on **High** for 4 to 6 hours, until bubbling and heated through. Serve with sour cream.

Magnificent Meatloaf

Serves 4 to 6

TIP

I am convinced there is no better way to cook meatloaf than in a slow cooker. Slow cooking helps keep it juicy and moist, and makes for easy cutting too. This loaf can be made with 2 lbs (1 kg) ground beef (instead of the beef and pork) or you can use 1 lb (500 g) beef and substitute ground chicken or turkey for the ground pork.

MENU SUGGESTION

Magnificent Meatloaf
Mashed Potatoes
Baby Carrots
Apple Crisp

1 lb	lean ground beef	500 g
1 lb	lean ground pork	500 g
4	green onions, finely chopped	4
1	pkg (10 oz [300 g]) frozen chopped spinach, thawed and drained	1
3/4 cup	fine dry breadcrumbs	175 mL
1/2 cup	grated Parmesan cheese	125 mL
1/4 cup	chili sauce	50 mL
2	eggs, lightly beaten	2
1/4 cup	finely chopped parsley (or 2 tbsp [25 mL] dried)	50 mL
2 tsp	salt	10 mL
1/2 tsp	ground nutmeg	2 mL
1/4 tsp	black pepper	1 mL
	Chopped fresh parsley	

1. Fold a 2-foot (60 cm) piece of aluminum foil in half lengthwise twice. Place on bottom and up the sides of slow cooker liner.

2. In a large bowl, combine beef and pork, mixing well. In a separate bowl, combine green onions, spinach, breadcrumbs, cheese, chili sauce, eggs, parsley, salt, nutmeg and pepper. Add to meat and mix well. Press evenly into foil-lined slow cooker. Tuck ends of foil under lid.

3. Cover and cook on **Low** for 8 to 10 hours or on **High** for 4 to 6 hours, until juices run clear when meat loaf is pierced with a fork. Serve sprinkled with chopped fresh parsley.

Mediterranean Pot Roast

Serves 6 to 8

I have fond memories of walking into my grandmother's house for Sunday night dinner and being greeted with the tantalizing aroma of a roast braising in the oven. This sophisticated version features tangy sun-dried tomatoes and olives served with a rich beef juice.

TIP

Choose a well-marbled roast such as cross rib, blade or rump.

Adding vinegar, apple juice or wine to a pot roast helps tenderize the meat while it simmers.

MENU SUGGESTION

Mediterranean Pot Roast
Mashed Potatoes
Steamed Green Beans
Apple Pie

☾ NIGHT BEFORE ·

This dish can be completely assembled up to 12 hours in advance of cooking. Follow preparation directions and refrigerate overnight in the slow cooker stoneware. The next day, place stoneware in slow cooker and continue cooking as directed.

1 tbsp	vegetable oil	15 mL
1 tbsp	dried Italian seasoning	15 mL
1	large clove garlic, minced	1
1	3- to 4-lb (1.5 to 2 kg) cross rib or blade roast	1
1 tsp	black pepper	5 mL
1/3 cup	sun-dried tomatoes (packed in oil), drained and chopped	75 mL
1/2 cup	pitted black olives, halved	125 mL
10 to 12	pearl onions, peeled	10 to 12
1/2 cup	beef stock	125 mL
1 tbsp	balsamic vinegar	15 mL

1. In a large skillet, heat oil over medium-high heat. Add Italian seasoning and garlic; cook for 1 minute. Sprinkle roast with pepper and place in hot seasoned oil. Cook, turning with a wooden spoon, for 7 to 10 minutes or until brown on all sides. Transfer meat to slow cooker.

2. Sprinkle roast with sun-dried tomatoes, olives and onions. In a bowl combine stock and vinegar and pour into slow cooker. Cover and cook on **Low** for 8 to 10 hours or on **High** for 4 to 6 hours.

3. Remove beef from slow cooker and let stand for 15 minutes before serving. To slice beef, cut across the grain. Serve with beef juice and vegetables.

Homestyle Pot Roast

Serves 6 to 8

I make this pot roast when I want to be reminded of my childhood and the wonderful aromas that greeted me when I walked in the door. I'm sure my children will have similar memories when they get older.

TIP

Slow cooking helps to tenderize less expensive cuts of meat. Pot roast benefits from a longer cooking on **Low**, but if you're short of time, count on 6 hours of simmering on **High** to produce fork-tender meat.

◑ NIGHT BEFORE

This dish can be completely assembled up to 12 hours in advance of cooking. Follow preparation directions and refrigerate overnight in the slow cooker stoneware. The next day, place stoneware in slow cooker and continue cooking as directed.

1/4 cup	all-purpose flour	50 mL
	Salt and black pepper	
1	3- to 4-lb (1.5 to 2 kg) beef cross rib or rump roast	1
1 tbsp	vegetable oil	15 mL
2	onions, quartered	2
4	carrots, peeled and sliced	4
4 to 6	potatoes, peeled and quartered	4 to 6
1 cup	beef stock	250 mL
1	small can (7.5 oz [221 mL]) tomato sauce	1
1	clove garlic, minced	1
1/2 tsp	dried thyme	2 mL
1	bay leaf	1
	Salt and pepper	

1. In a bowl season flour to taste with salt and pepper. Pat meat dry and coat on all sides with seasoned flour.

2. In a large skillet, heat oil over medium-high heat. Add meat and cook, turning with a wooden spoon, for 7 to 10 minutes or until brown on all sides. Transfer meat to slow cooker.

3. Add onions to slow cooker, along with carrots, potatoes, stock, tomato sauce, garlic, thyme and bay leaf. Cover and cook on **Low** for 10 to 12 hours or on **High** for 6 to 8 hours, until vegetables are tender.

4. Remove roast, onions, carrots and potatoes, cover and set aside. Discard bay leaf. Tip slow cooker and skim off any excess fat from surface of gravy; season to taste with salt and pepper. Pour gravy into sauceboat. Slice roast, arrange on a serving platter and surround with vegetables. Serve with gravy.

Osso Buco with Lemon Gremolata

Serves 6 to 8

This classic Italian dish is perfect for the slow cooker. It needs long slow, all-day cooking – just what you need for easy entertaining. Your guests will be greeted with a tantalizing aroma when they walk through the door!

TIP

I recommend you use a large (5- to 6-quart) slow cooker to make this recipe. For a smaller (2 1/2- to 4-quart) slow cooker, reduce ingredients by half and use a 19-oz [540 mL] can of tomatoes.

Veal shanks are readily available in the fresh meat section of the supermarket. It's important to secure them with butcher's twine so they won't fall apart while cooking. Ask the butcher to do this for you – it will save you some extra work at home.

8	thick slices veal shank, each tied with string	8
	Salt and black pepper	
	All-purpose flour	
2 tbsp	olive oil	25 mL
2 tbsp	butter	25 mL
2	medium onions, finely chopped	2
2	carrots, peeled and finely chopped	2
1	stalk celery, finely chopped	1
6	large cloves garlic, minced	6
1 cup	dry white wine	250 mL
3/4 cup	chicken or beef stock	175 mL
1	can (28 oz [796 mL]) tomatoes, drained and chopped	1
2	whole fresh basil leaves (or 1/2 tsp [2 mL] dried)	2
2	whole fresh thyme sprigs (or 1/2 tsp [2 mL] dried)	2
1/4 cup	chopped fresh parsley (or 2 tbsp [25 mL] dried)	50 mL
2	bay leaves	2

GREMOLATA

1 tbsp	grated lemon zest	15 mL
1	clove garlic, minced	1
1/4 cup	chopped fresh parsley	50 mL

1. Lightly sprinkle veal shanks on both sides with salt and pepper. Coat on both sides with flour, shaking off the excess.
2. In a large skillet, heat olive oil over medium-high heat. Add veal and cook until brown on both sides. Transfer veal to slow cooker. Pour off any excess fat from skillet.

3. Return skillet to medium heat and melt butter. Add onions, carrots, celery and garlic. Sauté for 5 minutes or until vegetables are softened. Add wine, stock, tomatoes, basil, thyme, parsley and bay leaves; stir to combine. Spoon over veal in slow cooker. Season to taste with salt and pepper.

4. Cover and cook on **Low** for 8 to 12 hours or on **High** for 5 to 7 hours, basting occasionally. Remove bay leaves and discard. If cooking on **High**, heat can be reduced to **Low** once meat has cooked the recommended length of time. The slow cooker will keep meat warm until ready to serve.

5. Gremolata: In a bowl combine lemon zest, garlic and parsley. When shanks are tender, remove strings and transfer to a warm platter. Spoon sauce over meat and sprinkle with gremolata garnish.

Philly Beef Wraps

Serves 4 to 6

This is a great way to use up any leftover shredded beef. Just warm it in the sauce and enjoy this no fuss, make-your-own dinner.

To serve, set out bowls of cheese, onions and hot pepper rings and let everyone help themselves.

To warm tortillas, wrap in foil and place in a 350° F (180° C) oven for 15 to 20 minutes.

How to fill and fold tortillas. Spoon filling onto warm tortilla. Fold over right side of tortilla. Fold bottom of tortilla. Fold left side over and serve.

2 lbs	warm cooked shredded beef (from COMFORTING SHREDDED BEEF, see recipe, page 94)	1 kg
8	large flour tortillas	8
8	slices Provolone or Swiss cheese	8
	Cooked onion slices	
	Pickled hot pepper rings	

1. Spoon shredded beef into center of each warm flour tortilla. Top with cooked onions (from slow cooker), one cheese slice and a few pepper rings. Fold into a package shape. (See Tip, lower left.)
2. Serve with warm cooking juice for dipping.

Oxford Beef with Mushrooms

Serves 4

This delicious stew is similar to Beef Bourguignonne, but with added sweetness from the jam.

TIP

For a jewel-like appearance, add chopped dried apricots halfway through the cooking.

Browning seasoned meat before it is placed in the slow cooker will give the stew an extra-rich flavor. But if you're pressed for time, you can dredge the meat in flour and add it directly to the slow cooker without browning first.

MAKE AHEAD

Cooking this stew the day before will give the flavors a chance to mingle and mellow.

MENU SUGGESTION

Oxford Beef with Mushrooms
Mashed Potatoes
Baked Squash
Sliced Bananas and Milk

1/4 cup	all-purpose flour	50 mL
1 tsp	salt	5 mL
1/2 tsp	black pepper	2 mL
2 lbs	stewing beef, cut into 1-inch (2.5 cm) pieces	1 kg
2 tbsp	vegetable oil	25 mL
1	large onion, sliced	1
2	cloves garlic, minced	2
8 oz	sliced mushrooms	250 g
1/2 cup	apricot jam	125 mL
1/2 cup	red wine	125 mL
1 cup	beef stock	250 mL
1	green or red bell pepper, sliced	1

1. In a bowl or plastic bag, combine flour, salt and pepper. In batches, toss beef to coat with flour mixture. Transfer to a plate.

2. In a large skillet, heat half the oil over medium-high heat. Cook beef in batches, adding more oil as needed until browned all over. Transfer beef to slow cooker. Add onion, garlic and mushrooms.

3. In a bowl combine jam, wine and stock; add to slow cooker stirring to combine. Cover and cook on **Low** for 8 to 10 hours or on **High** for 4 to 6 hours.

4. Before serving, add sliced peppers. Cover and cook on **High** for another 15 to 20 minutes.

St. Patty's Corned Beef and Veggies with Marmalade-Mustard Glaze

Serves 8 to 10

BAKING SHEET

4 to 6	potatoes, peeled and quartered	4 to 6
4 to 6	carrots, peeled and cut into 2-inch [5 cm] chunks	4 to 6
2	onions, cut into quarters	2
1	4-lb (2 kg) corned beef brisket	1
1	bottle (12 oz [341 mL]) strong beer	1
2 to 4	whole cloves	2 to 4
1 tsp	whole peppercorns	5 mL
1 tbsp	brown sugar	15 mL
	Water	
1	small cabbage, cut into wedges	1

MARMALADE GLAZE

1/2 cup	orange marmalade	125 mL
2 tbsp	Dijon mustard	25 mL
2 tbsp	brown sugar	25 mL

1. In slow cooker, combine potatoes, carrots and onions. Add corned beef, beer, cloves, pepper-corns and brown sugar. Pour in enough water to cover meat and vegetables.

2. Cover and cook on **Low** for 10 to 12 hours or on **High** for 6 to 8 hours. Remove meat from cooking liquid and place on baking sheet. Transfer vegetables to a platter and keep warm.

3. Pour cooking liquid into a large pot over medium-high heat. Taste and, if too salty, discard some of the liquid and replace it with fresh water. Repeat until saltiness is to your taste. Secure cabbage wedges with toothpicks and add to cooking liquid. Bring liquid to a boil; reduce heat and simmer for 15 minutes or until cabbage is tender.

4. Marmalade Glaze: In a bowl combine marmalade, mustard and brown sugar. Spoon over corned beef and place under a preheated broiler, 6 inches (15 cm) from heat source. Cook for about 2 to 3 minutes.

5. Thinly slice beef against the grain and place on platter with vegetables. Add cabbage wedges to platter and serve with additional mustard.

Texas-Style Barbecued Brisket Sandwiches

Serves 6 to 8

Brisket, a less tender cut of beef, is extremely well suited to slow cooking. This down-home favorite recipe uses hickory-flavored barbecue sauce which adds a rich, smoky flavor. It is best cooked long and slow.

TIP

Serve this perfect picnic fare with BEST-EVER BAKED BEANS (see recipe, page 73), which can be made the day before and eaten cold.

MENU SUGGESTION

TEXAS-STYLE BARBECUED
 BRISKET SANDWICHES
Potato Salad
BEST-EVER BAKED BEANS
 (see recipe, page 73)

1	3-lb (1.5 kg) brisket point roast, well-trimmed	1
1/2 cup	ketchup	125 mL
1/4 cup	water	50 mL
1/4 cup	honey	50 mL
1/4 cup	red wine vinegar	50 mL
2 tbsp	brown sugar	25 mL
2 tbsp	hot pepper sauce (or 1 tsp [5 mL] red pepper flakes)	25 mL
2 tbsp	hickory-flavored barbecue sauce	25 mL
1 tbsp	Worcestershire sauce	15 mL
1 tbsp	Dijon mustard	15 mL
1 tbsp	soya sauce	15 mL
2	cloves garlic, minced	2
1	onion, finely chopped	1
8	kaiser buns, split	8

1. Place brisket in slow cooker. (If meat is too large for your slow cooker, cut crosswise into 2 or 3 chunks.)

2. In a large bowl or glass measure, combine ketchup, water, honey, vinegar, sugar, hot pepper sauce, barbecue sauce, Worcestershire sauce, mustard, soya sauce, garlic and onion. Mix well and pour over brisket. Cover and cook on **Low** for 8 to 10 hours, until meat is very tender.

3. Remove meat from slow cooker and let stand for 10 minutes before carving. Using a sharp knife, slice meat across the grain into thin slices. Place meat on one kaiser half, add 1 tbsp (25 mL) sauce and cover with other kaiser half. Serve with additional sauce for dipping.

Three-Cheese Meatloaf

Serves 4 to 6

If you can't imagine serving meatloaf to guests, try this one. With all the cheese, even the kids will love it! Make sure you serve it hot so the cheese still bubbles.

MENU SUGGESTION

THREE-CHEESE MEATLOAF
Mashed Potatoes
Steamed Green Beans
Warm Apple Crisp with Ice Cream

2 lbs	lean ground beef	1 kg
1	large onion, finely chopped	1
Half	green pepper, finely chopped	Half
1/2 cup	fine dry breadcrumbs	125 mL
1 tsp	salt	5 mL
1/2 tsp	black pepper	2 mL
1/2 tsp	paprika	2 mL
2	eggs, lightly beaten	2
1/4 cup	milk	50 mL
1 tsp	dried Italian seasoning	5 mL
1/3 cup	diced mozzarella cheese (1/2-inch [1 cm] cubes)	75 mL
1/3 cup	diced Swiss cheese (1/2-inch [1 cm] cubes)	75 mL
1/2 cup	freshly grated Parmesan cheese	125 mL

1. Fold a 2-ft (60 cm) piece of aluminum foil lengthwise in half twice. Place on bottom and up sides of slow cooker.

2. In a large bowl, combine beef, onion, green pepper, breadcrumbs, salt, pepper and paprika, mixing well. In a small bowl, combine eggs and milk; stir into meat mixture. Add Italian seasoning, mozzarella, Swiss and Parmesan cheeses. Using your hands, blend meat mixture well and press into foil-lined slow cooker. Tuck ends of foil under lid.

3. Cover and cook on **Low** for 8 to 10 hours or on **High** for 4 to 6 hours, until juices run clear when meatloaf is pierced with a fork and cheese is bubbling. Serve immediately.

Burgundy Beef and Wild Mushroom Stew

Serves 4 to 6

If you love the combination of beef and mushrooms, this stew is sure to be one of your favorites.

There are many types of dried mushrooms, including varieties such as shiitake and chanterelles. When they are properly rehydrated, their flavor and texture are as good as fresh. And if the soaking liquid is incorporated into the recipe, it adds even more flavor. Besides hot water, you can try using red wine or beef stock to soak the mushrooms for this stew.

For an extra-peppery flavor, try adding the optional freshly cracked black peppercorns to the flour used for dredging the beef.

1	pkg (5 oz [142 g]) dried mushrooms, such as shiitake or chanterelles	1
1 cup	boiling water	250 mL
1/4 cup	all-purpose flour	50 mL
2 tsp	freshly cracked black pepper (optional)	10 mL
1/2 tsp	dried basil	2 mL
1/2 tsp	dried oregano	2 mL
1/2 tsp	salt	2 mL
2 lbs	stewing beef, cut into 1-inch (2.5 cm) cubes	500 g
2 tbsp	vegetable oil	25 mL
1 cup	beef stock	250 mL
2	medium carrots, peeled and cut lengthwise in half, then crosswise into thirds	2
1	onion, chopped *or* 15 to 20 pearl onions, peeled	1
2	cloves garlic, minced	2
8 oz	button mushrooms, quartered	250 g
1/2 cup	red wine	125 mL
2 tbsp	tomato paste	25 mL
1 tbsp	balsamic vinegar	15 mL
1	bay leaf	1

1. In a 2-cup (500 mL) measuring cup, combine dried mushrooms and boiling water. Let stand for 20 to 30 minutes.

2. In a heavy plastic bag, combine flour, pepper (if using), basil, oregano and salt. In batches, add beef to flour mixture and toss to coat. Transfer to a plate. In a large nonstick skillet, heat half the oil over medium-high heat; cook beef in batches, adding more oil as needed, until browned all over. With a slotted spoon, transfer beef to slow cooker. Add beef stock to pan; stir to scrape up brown bits and transfer to slow cooker.

3. Add carrots to slow cooker, along with onion, garlic, button mushrooms, wine, tomato paste, vinegar and bay leaf.

4. With a slotted spoon, remove rehydrated mush-rooms from soaking liquid; coarsely chop and add to slow cooker along with soaking liquid; stir well to combine beef-vegetable mixture.

5. Cover and cook on **Low** for 8 to 10 hours or on **High** for 4 to 6 hours, until vegetables are tender and stew is bubbling. Remove bay leaf and discard before serving.

Coconut Beef Curry

Serves 6 to 8

TIP

Red curry paste is often available in the oriental food section of the supermarket. It is popular in Indian and Thai dishes and adds a wonderful zing to most recipes. If you can't find it, use curry powder instead.

Serve this dish over hot cooked couscous or basmati rice.

Canned coconut milk is made from grated and soaked coconut pulp – not, as you might think, from the liquid found inside the coconut. It can be found in the oriental foods section of most supermarkets or Asian food stores. Be sure you don't buy coconut cream, which is often used for making tropical drinks such as pina coladas.

1 tbsp	vegetable oil	15 mL
2 lbs	stewing beef, cut into 1/4-inch (3 mm) strips	1 kg
2	onions, sliced	2
2	cloves garlic, minced	2
2 tbsp	paprika	25 mL
2 tbsp	ground cumin	25 mL
1 tsp	cinnamon	5 mL
2 tsp	red curry paste *or* 1 tbsp (15 mL) curry powder	10 mL
4	medium potatoes, peeled and chopped	4
1	bag (1 lb [500 g]) peeled baby carrots	1
2 tbsp	tomato paste	25 mL
1	can (14 oz [398 mL]) coconut milk	1
1/2 cup	water	125 mL
1 tsp	salt	5 mL
	Chopped fresh cilantro	

1. In a large nonstick skillet, heat oil over medium-high heat. In batches, add beef strips and cook for 2 to 3 minutes per batch or until browned on all sides. Add onions, garlic, paprika, cumin, cinnamon and curry paste (or curry powder). Sauté for 2 minutes or until fragrant. With a slotted spoon, transfer mixture to slow cooker. Add potatoes and carrots.
2. In a small bowl, combine tomato paste, coconut milk, water and salt; mix well. Add to slow cooker; stir to combine with meat and vegetables.
3. Cover and cook on **Low** for 8 to 10 hours or on **High** for 4 to 6 hours, until vegetables are tender and stew is bubbling. Serve sprinkled with cilantro.

Mediterranean Veal Stew

Serves 4 to 6

Impress your dinner guests with this delicately flavored veal stew.

TIP

For an authentic Mediterranean flavor, serve with a Greek salad (chopped tomatoes, cucumbers and black olives, tossed with a lemon-oregano vinaigrette).

Veal is sold in milk-fed or grain-fed varieties. Milk-fed veal has a soft creamy pink color and is considered superior. Grain-fed veal is redder but is still delicately flavored. For convenience, look for pre-cut cubes of stewing veal. If you can't get veal, use stewing beef instead.

☾ NIGHT BEFORE

This dish can be completely assembled up to 12 hours in advance of cooking. Follow preparation directions and refrigerate overnight in the slow cooker stoneware. The next day, place stoneware in slow cooker and continue cooking as directed.

1/4 cup	all-purpose flour	50 mL
2 tsp	dried oregano	10 mL
1/2 tsp	dried thyme	2 mL
1 tsp	salt	5 mL
1/4 tsp	black pepper	1 mL
2 lbs	veal shoulder or leg, well-trimmed and cut into 1-inch (2.5 cm) cubes	1 kg
2 tbsp	vegetable oil	25 mL
1 cup	chicken stock	250 mL
2	cloves garlic, minced	2
1	medium onion, chopped	1
1	small can (7.5 oz [221 mL]) tomato sauce	1
2 tbsp	red wine vinegar	25 mL
1/4 cup	sun-dried tomatoes (packed, in oil), drained and chopped	50 mL
1	green pepper, coarsely chopped	1
1/2 cup	crumbled feta cheese	125 mL
2 tbsp	chopped fresh parsley	25 mL

1. In a heavy plastic bag, combine flour, oregano, thyme, salt and pepper. In batches, add veal to flour mixture and toss to coat. Transfer to a plate. In a large nonstick skillet, heat half the oil over medium-high heat. Cook veal in batches, adding more oil as needed, until browned all over. With a slotted spoon, transfer veal to slow cooker.

2. Add stock to pan and stir to scrape up any brown bits. Transfer stock mixture to slow cooker, along with garlic, onion, tomato sauce, vinegar and sun-dried tomatoes. Cover and cook on **Low** for 8 to 10 hours or on **High** for 4 to 6 hours, until meat is tender and stew is bubbling.

3. Stir in green pepper. Cover and cook on **High** for 15 to 20 minutes or until heated through. Spoon stew into individual serving bowls and top each with crumbled feta cheese and parsley.

113

Mom's Old-Fashioned Beef Stew

Serves 6 to 8

This stew is just like one my mother used to make when my sisters and I were little girls and she was the busy mom-on-the-run.

TIP

Serve with thick slices of crusty bread to soak up every last drop of the rich gravy.

Store any leftovers in the refrigerator up to 3 days or freeze for up to 3 months. For best consistency, add 1/2 cup (125 mL) water before reheating.

VARIATION

For a slight change of pace, I sometimes make this stew with a can of chunky-style tomatoes with roasted garlic and basil.

🌙 NIGHT BEFORE

This dish can be completely assembled up to 12 hours in advance of cooking. Follow preparation directions and refrigerate overnight in the slow cooker stoneware. The next day, place stoneware in slow cooker and continue cooking as directed.

1/4 cup	all-purpose flour	50 mL
1 tsp	salt	5 mL
1/2 tsp	black pepper	2 mL
2 lbs	stewing beef, cut into 1/2-inch (1 cm) cubes	1 kg
2 tbsp	vegetable oil	25 mL
2 cups	beef stock	500 mL
4	medium carrots, peeled and sliced	4
4	medium potatoes, peeled and chopped	4
2	stalks celery, chopped	2
1	large onion, diced *or* 15 to 20 white pearl onions, peeled	1
1	can (19 oz [540 mL]) tomatoes, diced, with juice	1
1	bay leaf	1
1 tbsp	Worcestershire sauce	15 mL
1/4 cup	chopped fresh parsley (or 2 tbsp [25 mL] dried)	50 mL
1 cup	frozen peas	250 mL
	Salt and pepper	

1. In a heavy plastic bag, combine flour, salt and pepper. In batches, add beef to flour mixture and toss to coat. Transfer to a plate. In a large nonstick skillet, heat half the oil over medium-high heat. Cook beef in batches, adding more oil as needed, until browned all over. With a slotted spoon, transfer beef to a slow cooker.

2. Add 1 cup (250 mL) stock to pan and stir to scrape up any brown bits. Transfer stock mixture to slow cooker. Add carrots, potatoes, celery, onion, tomatoes (with juice), remaining stock, bay leaf, Worcestershire sauce and parsley; mix well to combine. Cover and cook on **Low** for 8 to 10 hours or on **High** for 4 to 6 hours, until vegetables are tender and stew is bubbling. Remove bay leaf and discard.

3. Add peas. Cover and cook on **High** 15 to 20 minutes longer or until slightly thickened and peas are heated through. Season to taste with salt and pepper.

Zesty Orange Beef Stew

Serves 4 to 6

This tasty stew gets its name from both the orange zest and the colorful fall vegetables.

For greater ease of preparation, look for pre-cut squash in the produce department of the supermarket.

Refrigerating any leftover stew always improves the flavor (which is why it always tastes better the next day). The fat will rise to the top and solidify; remove it before reheating.

NIGHT BEFORE

This dish can be completely assembled up to 12 hours in advance of cooking. Follow preparation directions and refrigerate overnight in the slow cooker stoneware. The next day, place stoneware in slow cooker and continue cooking as directed.

1/4 cup	all-purpose flour	50 mL
1 tsp	salt	5 mL
1/2 tsp	black pepper	2 mL
2 lbs	stewing beef, cut into 1-inch (2.5 cm) cubes	1 kg
2 tbsp	vegetable oil	25 mL
2 cups	beef stock	500 mL
2	onions, chopped	2
2	large carrots, peeled and chopped	2
2 cups	butternut squash, peeled and cut into 1 1/2-inch (3.5 cm) cubes	500 mL
4	medium potatoes, peeled and chopped	4
1 cup	red wine	250 mL
2 tbsp	tomato paste	25 mL
1/4 cup	fresh chopped parsley (or 2 tbsp [25 mL]) dried)	50 mL
1 tsp	grated orange zest	5 mL
1 tsp	dried rosemary leaves	5 mL
	Chopped fresh parsley	

1. In a heavy plastic bag, combine flour, salt and pepper. In batches, add beef to flour mixture and toss to coat. Transfer to a plate. In a large nonstick skillet, heat half the oil over medium-high heat. Cook beef in batches, adding more oil as needed, until browned all over. With a slotted spoon, transfer beef to slow cooker.
2. Add 1 cup (250 mL) stock to skillet and stir to scrape up any brown bits. Transfer stock mixture to slow cooker. Add onions, carrots, squash and potatoes.
3. In a bowl combine red wine, remaining stock, tomato paste, parsley, orange zest and rosemary. Pour over vegetables in slow cooker and mix well to combine. Cover and cook on **Low** for 8 to 10 hours or on **High** for 4 to 6 hours. Serve garnished with chopped fresh parsley.

Pork & Lamb

Calcutta Lamb Curry

Serves 4 to 6

TIP

Accompany this sweet and flavorful curry with additional sweet mango chutney and a selection of condiments – chopped green onions, chopped peanuts and toasted coconut. It's best served on a bed of sweet-scented basmati, a long grain East Indian rice.

Mango chutney is found in the condiment section of most supermarkets.

Canned coconut milk is made from grated and soaked coconut pulp – not, as you might think, from the liquid found inside the coconut. It can be found in the oriental foods section of most supermarkets or Asian food stores. Be sure you don't buy coconut cream, which is often used for making tropical drinks such as pina coladas, and is far too sweet for curry.

1 tbsp	vegetable oil	15 mL
1	2-lb (1 kg) lamb shank or butt roast, well trimmed and cut into 1-inch (2.5 cm) cubes	1
2 tbsp	all-purpose flour	25 mL
2 tbsp	curry powder	25 mL
1/2 tsp	red pepper flakes	2 mL
1/2 tsp	paprika	2 mL
1/2 tsp	dried marjoram	2 mL
1 cup	chicken stock	250 mL
2	large Granny Smith apples, peeled, cored and coarsely chopped	2
2	stalks celery, coarsely chopped	2
2	onions, finely chopped	2
2	cloves garlic, minced	2
1 tbsp	minced ginger root	15 mL
1	can (14 oz [398 mL]) coconut milk	1
1 tsp	salt	5 mL
1/4 cup	mango chutney	50 mL
1/2 cup	raisins	125 mL
1/3 cup	yogurt *or* sour cream	75 mL
1 tsp	grated lemon zest	5 mL

1. In a large nonstick skillet, heat oil over medium-high heat. Add lamb and cook for 6 to 8 minutes or until browned.
2. In a small bowl, combine flour, curry powder, red pepper flakes, paprika and marjoram. Sprinkle over lamb cubes, tossing to coat well.
3. Add stock to skillet and cook, scraping up brown bits from bottom of skillet. Bring to a boil, reduce heat and simmer for about 5 minutes.

NIGHT BEFORE

This dish can be assembled up to 12 hours in advance. Prepare the ingredients as directed up to the cooking stage, (but without adding chutney, raisins and lemon zest), and refrigerate in stoneware insert overnight. The next day, place stoneware in slow cooker and continue cooking as directed.

4. Transfer meat mixture to slow cooker. Add apples, celery, onions, garlic, ginger root, coconut milk and salt. Cover and cook on **Low** for 8 to 10 hours or on **High** for 4 to 6 hours, until meat is tender.

5. Transfer curry to a serving dish. Stir in chutney, raisins, yogurt and lemon zest. Serve immediately.

Southern Barbecued Pork on a Bun

Serves 8

This is perfect picnic fare – easy to make ahead (see below) and serve to appreciative family and friends in the great outdoors.

MAKE AHEAD

Marinate the pork up to 24 hours in advance. Cook meat overnight in slow cooker, slice, then return it to the warm sauce. Wrap the removable insert with towels and secure lid with elastic bands, then pack in a tight box. Take to the picnic and serve immediately.

MENU SUGGESTION

SOUTHERN BARBECUED PORK
  ON A BUN
Corn-on-the-Cob
Creamy Coleslaw
S'mores

1 cup	ketchup	250 mL
1 cup	chili sauce (homemade or store bought)	250 mL
1/4 cup	Dijon mustard	50 mL
2 tbsp	cider vinegar *or* white vinegar	25 mL
1 tbsp	Worcestershire sauce	15 mL
1/2 tsp	red pepper flakes	2 mL
4	cloves garlic, minced	4
1	3-lb (1.5 kg) boneless pork shoulder butt roast, trimmed of excess fat	1
8	kaiser buns, split	8

1. In a saucepan over medium-high heat, combine ketchup, chili sauce, mustard, vinegar, Worcestershire sauce, red pepper flakes and garlic. Bring mixture to a boil, reduce heat and simmer 5 minutes. Let cool.

2. Place roast in a large glass bowl or resealable plastic bag. Pour sauce over pork and marinate overnight in the refrigerator.

3. Remove roast from marinade and place in slow cooker. Add 3/4 cup (175 mL) water to marinade, mix well and add to roast in slow cooker. Cover and cook on **Low** for 8 to 10 hours or on **High** for 4 to 6 hours, until meat is tender.

4. Remove meat from barbecue sauce and let stand 10 to 15 minutes before carving into thin slices. Place meat on one half of kaiser bun, add additional barbecue sauce and top with other half of bun.

Easy Jambalaya

Serves 6 to 8

This one-pot wonder origi-
nates from the deep South –
New Orleans, in fact – and
traditionally features a mix
of chicken, sausage and
shrimp. This scaled-down
version uses only ham and
shrimp, but still packs a
piquant punch. All you need
is a crisp garden salad to top
it off.

TIP

You can replace the ham with
any spicy sausage, such as
andouille, chorizo or hot
Italian.

Try replacing the canned
tomato sauce with 2 cups
(500 mL) Fia's Favorite Pasta
Sauce (see recipe page 78).

☾ NIGHT BEFORE

Jambalaya can be assembled
12 hours in advance. Prepare
the ingredients in the slow
cooker up to the cooking
stage (but without adding the
shrimp and green pepper)
and refrigerate in stoneware
insert overnight. The next
day, place stoneware in slow
cooker and continue cooking
as directed.

1	large onion, finely chopped	1
2	stalks celery, finely chopped	2
3	cloves garlic, minced	3
1	can (19 oz [540 mL]) plum tomatoes, diced, with juice	1
1	can (14 oz [398 mL]) tomato sauce	1
2 cups	chopped ham	500 mL
2 tbsp	dried parsley	25 mL
1 tsp	dried thyme	5 mL
1/2 tsp	salt	2 mL
1/2 tsp	red pepper flakes	2 mL
1/4 tsp	black pepper	1 mL
12 oz	medium shrimp, uncooked, peeled and deveined	375 g
1	medium green pepper, coarsely chopped	1
	Hot cooked rice	

1. In slow cooker, combine onion, celery, garlic, tomatoes (with juice), tomato sauce, ham, parsley, thyme, salt, red pepper flakes and black pepper.
2. Cover and cook on **Low** for 6 to 8 hours or on **High** for 3 to 4 hours, until vegetables are tender.
3. Add shrimp and green pepper; cover and cook on **Low** for another 15 to 20 minutes or until shrimp are pink and firm. Serve over hot rice.

Greek Lamb Loaf with Tzatziki Sauce

Serves 4

TIP

If you're pressed for time, buy pre-made tzatziki sauce; otherwise, prepare the sauce in this recipe right after you put the loaf in the slow cooker. As the loaf cooks, let the sauce sit, covered, in the refrigerator so it can develop its flavors.

MENU SUGGESTION

GREEK LAMB LOAF
Grilled Vegetables
Rice Pilaf
Baklava

☾ NIGHT BEFORE

This dish can be completely assembled up to 12 hours in advance of cooking. Follow preparation directions and refrigerate overnight in the slow cooker stoneware. The next day, place stoneware in slow cooker and continue cooking as directed.

2 lbs	ground lamb	1 kg
1/2 cup	fine dry breadcrumbs	125 mL
1	onion, finely chopped	1
2	cloves garlic, minced	2
1/2 cup	plain yogurt	125 mL
1 tbsp	lime juice	15 mL
1 tsp	ground coriander	5 mL
1 tsp	ground cumin	5 mL
1/2 tsp	red pepper flakes	2 mL
1/2 tsp	salt	2 mL
1	egg, lightly beaten	1

TZATZIKI SAUCE

1 cup	plain yogurt	250 mL
2	cloves garlic, minced	2
1 tsp	black pepper	5 mL
1 tsp	chopped fresh mint	5 mL

1. Fold a 2-foot (60 cm) piece of aluminum foil in half lengthwise twice, and place on bottom and up the sides of slow cooker liner.
2. In a large bowl, combine lamb, breadcrumbs, onion, garlic, yogurt, lime juice, coriander, cumin, red pepper flakes, salt and egg; mix well. Press mixture into prepared slow cooker.
3. Cover and cook on **Low** for 8 to 10 hours or on **High** for 4 to 6 hours. Remove loaf from slow cooker and let stand 5 minutes before slicing.
4. Tzatziki Sauce: In a bowl combine yogurt, garlic, pepper and mint; stir until well mixed. Refrigerate for at least 2 hours, then drizzle over loaf and serve.

Ham and Lentil Ragout

Serves 8

TIP

Lentils are a staple in Indian and Middle Eastern cooking. They come in three varieties – brown, red and green. I prefer green lentils for this dish, since they hold their shape well during the long slow-cooking process.

Serve with a crusty Italian buns and cold beer on the side.

VARIATION

For a livelier version of this dish, try using a spicy smoked sausage in place of the ham.

◑ NIGHT BEFORE

This dish can be completely assembled up to 12 hours in advance of cooking. Prepare the ingredients in the slow cooker up to the cooking stage (without adding the parsley) and refrigerate in stoneware. The next day, place stoneware in slow cooker and continue cooking as directed.

3 cups	chopped cooked ham	750 mL
2	carrots, peeled and finely chopped	2
2	stalks celery, finely chopped	2
1	onion, finely chopped	1
2 cups	dried green lentils	500 mL
2 cups	chicken stock	500 mL
4 cups	water	1 L
2 tsp	paprika	10 mL
1 tsp	dried thyme	5 mL
1/4 cup	chopped fresh parsley	50 mL

1. In slow cooker, combine ham, carrots, celery, onion, lentils, stock, water, paprika and thyme; mix well.
2. Cover and cook on **Low** for 6 to 8 hours or on **High** for 3 to 4 hours, until vegetables and lentils are tender. Stir in parsley and serve.

Country-Style Honey Garlic Ribs

Serves 4 as a main course or 10 as an appetizer

These sweet and tangy ribs are always a party hit. Have lots of napkins on hand for sticky fingers.

For added flavor, combine broiled ribs and sauce in a large bowl and marinate in the refrigerator for 1 hour. Transfer to slow cooker and proceed with Step 3.

To feed a larger (or hungrier!) crowd, double sauce ingredients and add 5 to 6 lbs (2.5 to 3 kg) ribs, cut in 2-rib portions.

Country-style ribs are the meatiest variety of pork ribs, but ordinary side ribs will also work in this recipe. To tenderize, cut ribs into 5- or 6-rib pieces and place in a large pot of water. Bring to a boil, reduce heat and simmer for 30 to 45 minutes.

PREHEAT BROILER
BAKING SHEET

3 lbs	Country-style pork ribs, cut into individual ribs	1.5 kg
	Freshly ground black pepper	
1 cup	prepared barbecue sauce (preferably smoke-flavored)	250 mL
1/2 cup	liquid honey	125 mL
1/4 cup	red wine vinegar	50 mL
4	cloves garlic, minced	4

1. Position broiler rack 6 inches (15 cm) from heat source. Place ribs on baking sheet and season well with pepper. Broil ribs, turning once, for 15 minutes or until browned. Drain and place ribs in slow cooker.

2. In a bowl combine barbecue sauce, honey, vinegar and garlic; stir well. Pour sauce over ribs in slow cooker.

3. Cover and cook, stirring ribs twice during cooking to coat well, on **Low** for 8 to 10 hours or on **High** for 4 to 6 hours, until ribs are tender and browned in sauce.

Pork Chops with Mixed Winter Fruit

Serves 4

Pork and dried fruit were made for one another, and here's the dish that proves it.

2 tsp	vegetable oil	10 mL
2 lbs	pork shoulder butt chops, trimmed	1 kg
1 cup	orange juice	250 mL
1 tsp	Worcestershire sauce	5 mL
1/2 tsp	ground ginger	2 mL
1/2 tsp	ground allspice	2 mL
1/2 tsp	cinnamon	2 mL
1	pkg (12 oz [375 g]) dried mixed fruit	1

1. In a skillet heat oil over medium-high heat. Add pork chops and cook 5 minutes per side or until browned. Remove chops and pat dry with paper towels to remove any excess oil.

2. Place in chops slow cooker. Add orange juice, Worcestershire sauce, ginger, allspice, cinnamon and dried fruit.

3. Cover and cook on **Low** for 7 to 9 hours or on **High** for 3 to 4 hours, until meat is tender. Serve pork chops with fruit spooned over top.

Roast Pork with Tangy Cranberry Sauce

Serves 6 to 8

TIP

If you can't find dried cranberries, use raisins instead.
The resulting sauce will be
sweeter (and less tangy) but
equally delicious.

There are three basic types of
pork roast – loin, leg and
shoulder. While loin roasts are
very lean and tender, they are
not the best for slow cooking.
A boneless shoulder butt
roast is ideal – it has some
marbling and is less tender,
which makes it perfect for all-
day, moist-heat cooking.

NIGHT BEFORE

This recipe can be assembled
12 to 24 hours in advance.
Prepare the ingredients in the
slow cooker up to the cooking
stage (without adding cornstarch and remaining 1/4 cup
[50 mL] cranberry juice) and
refrigerate in stoneware insert
overnight. The next day, place
stoneware in slow cooker and
continue cooking as directed.

MENU SUGGESTION

ROAST PORK WITH TANGY
  CRANBERRY SAUCE
Steamed Broccoli
Mixed Rice Pilaf
Whole Wheat Dinner Rolls

1	2- to 3-lb (1 to 1.5 kg) boneless pork shoulder butt roast	1
1 cup	dried cranberries	250 mL
1/2 cup	chicken stock	125 mL
1/2 cup	cranberry juice cocktail	125 mL
	Grated zest of half an orange	
1 tsp	ground ginger	5 mL
2 tbsp	cornstarch	25 mL
	Salt and black pepper to taste	

1. Place roast in a slow cooker. In a bowl combine cranberries, stock, 1/4 cup (50 mL) cranberry juice, orange zest and ginger, mixing well. Pour over roast. Cover and cook on **Low** for 6 to 10 hours or on **High** for 3 to 4 hours, until meat is tender.

2. Remove roast from slow cooker. Cover with foil to keep warm. Pour juices from slow cooker into a medium saucepan and skim off any accumulated fat.

3. In a small bowl, combine cornstarch with remaining 1/4 cup [50 mL] cranberry juice, stirring well to dissolve any lumps. Add to saucepan. Over medium-high heat, bring mixture to a boil, stirring constantly until thickened. Season to taste with salt and pepper and serve with roast pork.

Slow Cooker Cottage Roll

Serves 8

TIP

A cottage roll is the top end of the pork shoulder (otherwise known as the shoulder butt) and is cured in a brine. Its flavor is very similar to ham – but is much less expensive. It is just the right size for a slow cooker and available at most supermarkets in Canada – although not, unfortunately, in America.If you can't find a cottage roll, use ham instead.

MENU SUGGESTION

Slow Cooker Cottage Roll
Baked Sweet Potatoes
Steamed Brussels Sprouts
Baked Apples

1	3- to 3 1/2-lb (1.5 to 1.6 kg) pickled pork cottage roll *or* smoked ham	1
6	peppercorns	6
1	bay leaf	1
1	stalk celery, chopped	1
1	medium potato, peeled and diced	1
	Ginger ale *or* water	
	Grainy mustard	

1. If using cottage roll, remove plastic wrap (but not elastic string) and rinse to remove brine. Place cottage roll or ham in slow cooker. Add peppercorns, bay leaf, celery and potato. Add ginger ale to within 1 inch (2.5 cm) of top of slow cooker.

2. Cover and cook on **Low** for 8 to 10 hours or on **High** for 4 to 6 hours, until meat is tender and completely cooked.

3. Remove meat from slow cooker. Strain cooking liquid, discarding vegetables and seasonings. (Liquid can be used for making Black Bean Cassoulet Soup; see recipe, page 42.) Slice meat and serve with your favorite grainy mustard.

Spicy White Bean and Sausage Ragout

Serves 4

TIP

This dish packs plenty of heat. But if you're not a big fan of spicy food, use mild Italian sausage – it has lots of flavor, but without the zap. Serve with a crisp Caesar salad and a hearty red wine.

Use FIA'S FAVORITE PASTA SAUCE (see recipe, page 78) in place of store-bought pasta sauce.

Green peppers can become bitter if they are cooked too long. Adding them at the end of cooking allows them to soften slightly while preserving their sweet flavor.

1 lb	hot Italian sausages	500 g
2 cups	store-bought chunky-style pasta sauce	500 mL
1 cup	beef stock	250 mL
2	stalks celery, chopped	2
4	cloves garlic, minced	4
1 tsp	Italian seasoning	5 mL
2	cans (each 19 oz [540 mL]) white kidney beans, rinsed and drained *or* 4 cups (1 L) soaked, cooked and drained beans	2
1	green pepper, coarsely chopped	1

1. In a skillet over medium-high heat, cook sausages for 10 minutes or until browned on all sides. Cut into 1-inch (2.5 cm) slices.

2. Using a slotted spoon, transfer sausages to slow cooker. Add pasta sauce, stock, celery, garlic, Italian seasoning and kidney beans; stir to combine.

3. Cover and cook on **Low** for 6 to 7 hours or on **High** for 3 to 4 hours, until hot and bubbling. Stir in green pepper. Cover and cook for another 20 minutes before serving.

SOUTHERN BARBECUED PORK ON A BUN (PAGE 120) ➤

OVERLEAF: MEXICAN WEEKEND BRUNCH BAKE (PAGE 88) ➤

Winter Root and Sausage Casserole

Serves 4 to 6

1	large potato, peeled and cut into 1/2-inch (1 cm) cubes	1
1	large sweet potato, peeled and cut into 1/2-inch (1 cm) cubes	1
2	medium carrots, peeled and coarsely chopped	2
1	medium parsnip, peeled and coarsely chopped	1
1	medium onion, finely chopped	1
1 lb	smoked sausages, sliced	500 g
1	can (19 oz [540 mL]) pasta-style stewed tomatoes, with juice	1
1 1/2 cups	chicken stock	375 mL
2 tsp	granulated sugar	10 mL
1/2 tsp	dried thyme	2 mL
1/4 tsp	black pepper	1 mL
1/4 cup	chopped fresh parsley	50 mL

1. In slow cooker, combine potato, sweet potato, carrots, parsnip, onion, sausages, tomatoes (with juice), stock, sugar, thyme and pepper; stir to mix well.

2. Cover and cook on **Low** for 7 to 9 hours or on **High** for 3 to 4 hours, until vegetables are tender.

3. Stir in parsley during last 10 to 15 minutes of cooking time.

TIP

For a chill-chasing menu, serve this hearty casserole with thick slices of warm pumpernickel bread and mugs of hot orange-spice tea.

Parsnips are a wonderful winter vegetable that resemble white carrots. (At least that's the description I give my vegetable-wary children when they ask, "What's that?") Parsnips have a slightly sweet flavor and make a delicious addition to many soups and stews.

☽ NIGHT BEFORE

Casserole can be assembled 12 hours in advance. Prepare the ingredients in the slow cooker up to the cooking stage (without adding parsley) and refrigerate in stoneware insert overnight. The next day, place stoneware in slow cooker and continue cooking as directed.

MENU SUGGESTION

Winter Root and Sausage Casserole
Crisp Green Salad
Pumpernickel Bread
Baked Apples

◄ Mother Hubbard's Favorite Shepherd's Pie (Page 142)

South African Lamb Stew

Serves 6 to 8

My friend Gill Ireland hails from South Africa, where lamb is very much a staple. She passed this delicately flavored stew along to me and I have adapted it to the slow cooker.

TIP

Enjoy the stew with a hearty South African red wine and a thick, crusty loaf of bread.

The best cuts for lamb stew come from the shoulder or shank. Avoid using loin – it can be very expensive and overcooks quickly.

🌙 NIGHT BEFORE

Stew can be assembled 12 hours in advance. Prepare the ingredients in the slow cooker up to the cooking stage (without adding green peas, lemon zest and parsley) and refrigerate in stoneware insert overnight. The next day, place stoneware in slow cooker and continue cooking as directed.

1/4 cup	all-purpose flour	50 mL
1/2 tsp	salt	2 mL
1/4 tsp	black pepper	1 mL
1 lb	boneless lamb shoulder roast, trimmed and cut into 1-inch (2.5 cm) cubes	500 g
1 tbsp	vegetable oil	15 mL
1	large onion, chopped	1
3	carrots, peeled and chopped	3
3	large potatoes, peeled and chopped	3
1 1/2 cups	chopped rutabaga	375 mL
1	can (19 oz [540 mL]) tomatoes, chopped, with juice	1
2 cups	beef stock	500 mL
1 tbsp	soya sauce	15 mL
1 tsp	granulated sugar	5 mL
1 cup	frozen peas	250 mL
1 tbsp	grated lemon zest	15 mL
1 tbsp	chopped fresh parsley	15 mL

1. In a bowl or plastic bag, combine flour, salt and pepper. In batches, add lamb to flour mixture and toss to coat. Transfer to a plate. In a large nonstick skillet, heat oil over medium-high heat. Add lamb and cook for 4 to 5 minutes or until brown on all sides. With a slotted spoon transfer to slow cooker.

2. Add onion, carrots, potatoes, rutabaga, tomatoes (with juice), stock, soya sauce and sugar. Mix well to combine. Cover and cook on **Low** for 8 to 10 hours or on **High** for 4 to 6 hours, until vegetables are tender and stew is bubbling.

3. Add peas. Cover and cook on **High** for another 15 to 20 minutes.

4. Spoon into serving bowls and sprinkle with lemon zest and parsley.

Hungarian Pork Goulash

Serves 4 to 6

Don't be alarmed by the amount of paprika in this recipe. The large quantity adds a rich color to the sauce, but not a lot of spiciness. Omit the optional sauerkraut if you wish, but it gives this dish an authentic European character.

The most flavorful paprika hails from Hungary, where it can be anywhere from mild and sweet to fiery-hot. This recipe is based on the milder variety, so make sure you check the label on the paprika before you buy. If all you have is the hotter type of paprika, reduce the amount by half.

Try replacing canned sauerkraut with the fresh variety. It can generally be found in the fresh meat or deli department of the grocery store.

NIGHT BEFORE

Stew can be assembled 12 hours in advance. Prepare the ingredients in the slow cooker up to the cooking stage (without sour cream) and refrigerate in stoneware insert overnight. The next day, place stoneware in slow cooker and continue cooking as directed.

1 tbsp	vegetable oil	15 mL
2 lbs	boneless pork shoulder roast, cut into 1 1/2-inch (3.5 cm) cubes	1 kg
2	onions, sliced	2
2	cloves garlic, minced	2
1/4 cup	paprika	50 mL
1/2 tsp	salt	2 mL
1/2 tsp	black pepper	2 mL
1	can or jar (19 oz [540 mL]) sauerkraut, rinsed and drained (optional)	1
1	can (19 oz [540 mL]) tomatoes, chopped, with juice	1
1 cup	beef stock	250 mL
1 cup	light sour cream	250 mL
	Hot cooked egg noodles	
	Sour cream (optional)	

1. In a large nonstick skillet, heat oil over medium-high heat. Add pork cubes, onions and garlic; cook for 4 to 5 minutes or until brown on all sides. Sprinkle with paprika, salt and pepper; cook 1 minute longer.

2. With a slotted spoon, transfer pork and seasonings to slow cooker. Add sauerkraut (if using), tomatoes (with juice) and stock. Cover and cook on **Low** for 8 to 10 hours or on **High** for 4 to 6 hours, until meat is tender.

3. Reduce heat to **Low**. Stir in sour cream and cook 5 minutes longer. Serve over hot noodles. If desired, garnish with additional sour cream.

Pork and Parsnip Stew with Apricots

Serves 4 to 6

After many years of developing recipes for the pork industry, I'm convinced that fruit is just about the perfect accompaniment to any pork dish. Here, dried apricots, prunes and orange juice sweeten this savory stew.

TIP

When browning the meat in hot oil, avoid cooking too many cubes in the skillet at one time. The meat will steam rather than brown. Turn the meat frequently and remove with a slotted spoon as quickly as possible.

Adding a splash of balsamic vinegar to soups and stews helps to tenderize the meat and give it a sweet zing of flavor.

☾ NIGHT BEFORE

Stew can be assembled 12 hours in advance. Prepare the ingredients in the slow cooker up to the cooking stage (without adding apricots and prunes) and refrigerate in stoneware insert overnight. The next day, place stoneware in slow cooker and continue cooking as directed.

1/4 cup	all-purpose flour	50 mL
1/2 tsp	salt	2 mL
1/4 tsp	black pepper	2 mL
2 lbs	boneless pork shoulder butt roast, cut into 1-inch (2.5 cm) cubes	1 kg
1 tbsp	vegetable oil	15 mL
2	medium onions, finely chopped	2
2	large parsnips, peeled and cut into 1-inch (2.5 cm) slices	2
2	carrots, peeled and cut into 1-inch (2.5 cm) slices	2
1 1/2 cups	chicken stock	375 mL
1 cup	orange juice	250 mL
2 tbsp	balsamic vinegar	25 mL
1/2 tsp	ground allspice	2 mL
	Salt and black pepper to taste	
1/2 cup	dried apricots	125 mL
1/2 cup	pitted dried prunes	125 mL

1. In a bowl or plastic bag, combine flour, salt and pepper. In batches, add pork to flour mixture and toss to coat. Transfer to a plate. In a large nonstick skillet, heat oil over medium-high heat. Add seasoned pork and cook for 4 to 5 minutes or until browned on all sides.

2. With a slotted spoon, transfer pork to slow cooker. Add onions, parsnips, carrots, stock, orange juice, vinegar, allspice, salt and pepper; stir to combine.

3. Cover and cook on **Low** for 8 to 10 hours or on **High** for 4 to 6 hours, until vegetables are tender and stew is bubbling.

4. Add apricots and prunes. Cover and cook on **High** for another 15 to 20 minutes or until heated through. Season to taste with salt and pepper.

Poultry

Coq au vin

Serves 4 to 6

1	whole chicken, cut into parts (about 9 pieces)	1
1/4 cup	all-purpose flour	50 mL
8	slices bacon, chopped	8
2	onions, sliced	2
8 oz	small button mushrooms, cleaned	250 g
16	small new potatoes, scrubbed	16
4	cloves garlic, minced	4
1/4 cup	chopped fresh parsley (or 2 tbsp [25 mL] dried)	50 mL
1/2 tsp	dried thyme	2 mL
1	bay leaf	1
1/2 tsp	salt	2 mL
1/4 tsp	black pepper	1 mL
2 tbsp	brandy	25 mL
1 cup	red wine	250 mL
1 cup	chicken stock	250 mL

1. In a bowl dredge chicken pieces in flour and place in slow cooker.
2. In a skillet over medium heat, cook bacon until crisp. Drain on paper towels.
3. Transfer bacon to slow cooker. Add onions, mushrooms, potatoes, garlic, parsley, thyme, bay leaf, salt, pepper, brandy, wine and stock.
4. Cover and cook on **Low** for 6 to 8 hours, until juices run clear when chicken is pierced with a fork. Discard bay leaf before serving.

Basque Chicken

Enjoy the flavors of classic Spanish cooking in this easy-to-make chicken dish.

TIP

Serve over rice or mashed potatoes.

Cooking times for poultry may be longer for larger slow cookers and/or where there is a relatively high proportion of dark to white meat. For predominantly white-meat dishes, be sure to avoid overcooking.

☾ NIGHT BEFORE

Because the chicken is browned, this dish can be assembled the night before (but without adding peppers and olives.) Follow preparation directions and refrigerate overnight in slow cooker stoneware. The next day, place stoneware in slow cooker and continue cooking as directed.

MENU SUGGESTION

BASQUE CHICKEN
Rice
Green Salad

1/4 cup	all-purpose flour	50 mL
1/2 tsp	salt	2 mL
1/4 tsp	black pepper	1 mL
1/8 tsp	cayenne pepper	0.5 mL
4	chicken legs, separated into thighs and drumsticks (skin removed, if desired)	4
2 tbsp	vegetable oil	25 mL
2	onions, coarsely chopped	2
8	thin slices prosciutto, trimmed of of excess fat and chopped *or* shaved Black Forest ham	8
1	can (28 oz [796 mL]) tomatoes, drained and chopped	1
1	red bell pepper, coarsely chopped	1
1	green pepper, coarsely chopped	1
12	pitted black olives, halved	12

1. In a bowl or large plastic bag, combine flour, salt, pepper and cayenne pepper. In batches, coat chicken pieces with flour mixture.

2. In a large skillet, heat oil over medium-high heat. Cook chicken pieces in batches until browned all over. Transfer chicken to a slow cooker. Add onions, prosciutto and tomatoes.

3. Cover and cook on **Low** for 6 to 8 hours or on **High** for 4 to 6 hours, until juices run clear when chicken is pierced with a fork. Add red and green peppers. Cover and cook on **High** for another 20 to 25 minutes. Serve garnished with black olives.

Chicken-in-a-Pot

Serves 4 to 6

Kids love this simple poached chicken and so will you. It's tasty, simple and the ingredients take just minutes to prepare.

TIP

Serve chicken and sauce on a bed of rice.

If whole chicken is too large to fit into your slow cooker, cut it into pieces with a sharp knife.

Cooking times for poultry may be longer for larger slow cookers and/or where there is a relatively high proportion of dark to white meat. For pre-dominantly white-meat dishes, be sure to avoid overcooking.

VARIATION

For a more sophisticated version, replace Parsley Sauce with **Creamed Curry Sauce**: In saucepan melt butter with 1 tsp (5 mL) curry powder. Blend in flour and cook 1 minute, stirring constantly. Gradually whisk in 1 1/2 cups (375 mL) strained cooking liquid (from Step 3) and 1/2 cup (125 mL) whipping (35%) cream, stirring for 3 minutes or until sauce boils and thickens. Season to taste with salt and pepper.

1	roasting chicken (3 to 6 lbs [1.5 to 3 kg])	1
2 cups	chicken stock	500 mL
	Water to cover	
1	stalk celery, with leaves, cut in half	1
1	carrot, peeled and cut in half	1
1	small onion, peeled	1
1 tsp	salt	5 mL
6	whole black peppercorns	6
3 or 4	sprigs fresh parsley (or 1 tbsp [15 mL] dried)	3 or 4
2	sprigs whole fresh thyme (or 1/2 tsp [2 mL] dried)	2
2	whole cloves	2
1	small bay leaf	1

PARSLEY SAUCE

1/4 cup	butter *or* margarine	50 mL
1/4 cup	all-purpose flour	50 mL
2 cups	strained cooking liquid (from chicken) *or* chicken stock	500 mL
1/4 cup	chopped fresh parsley (or 2 tbsp [25 mL] dried)	50 mL
	Salt and black pepper	

1. Rinse chicken inside and out and pat dry. (Discard bag of giblets but reserve chicken neck, if desired.) Place chicken and, if using, neck into slow cooker. Pour in stock and add enough water to almost completely cover chicken, leaving 1 inch (2.5 cm) at top of slow cooker. Add celery, carrot, onion, salt, peppercorns, parsley, thyme, cloves and bay leaf.

2. Cover and cook on **Low** for 8 to 10 hours.

3. Carefully lift chicken from liquid and transfer to a plate; allow to rest for 15 to 20 minutes. Strain vegetables and cooking liquid, discarding vegetables and reserving liquid. Skim any fat from surface of liquid.

4. Parsley Sauce: In a saucepan over medium heat, melt butter. Blend in flour and cook for 1 minute, stirring constantly. Gradually whisk in strained cooking liquid, stirring for about 5 minutes or until sauce boils and thickens. Remove from heat and stir in parsley. Season to taste with salt and pepper. Serve sauce over chicken.

Drunken Roast Chicken

Serves 6 to 8

While roasting is something we typically associate with the oven, you can also "roast" in a slow cooker – with very tasty results. In this recipe, the garlic creates a wonderful aroma and imparts a subtle flavor to the chicken.

TIP

For a complete Sunday night dinner or easy weeknight meal, add chopped carrots and potatoes to the bottom of the slow cooker at the beginning of Step 3, then place chicken on top of vegetables and proceed with recipe as directed.

If you have thyme growing in your herb garden, substitute a few fresh sprigs for the dried thyme called for in this recipe.

If whole chicken is too large to fit in your slow cooker, cut it into pieces with a sharp knife.

Cooking times for poultry may be longer for larger slow cookers and/or where there is a relatively high proportion of dark to white meat. For predominantly white-meat dishes, be sure to avoid overcooking.

KITCHEN TWINE

1	roasting chicken (about 3 1/2 to 4 lbs [1.75 to 2 kg])	1
4 to 6	cloves garlic, halved	4 to 6
1	onion, quartered	1
1	stalk celery (with leaves), cut into 3 pieces	1
1 tsp	dried thyme	5 mL
1/2 tsp	paprika	2 mL
1/2 cup	chicken stock	125 mL
1/2 cup	dry white wine	125 mL
1 tbsp	Worcestershire sauce	15 mL

GRAVY

1 tbsp	butter	15 mL
1 tbsp	all-purpose flour	15 mL
	Salt and black pepper	

1. Rinse chicken inside and out and pat dry with paper towels. With your fingers, gently loosen skin from chicken breast to form a pocket. Insert garlic halves under the skin. Place onion and celery in the cavity.
2. With kitchen twine, tie chicken legs together and secure wings to body, leaving an extra length of twine at each end. You will use the ends to lift the chicken from slow cooker.
3. Place chicken in slow cooker, breast-side up. Sprinkle with thyme and paprika. Pour in stock, wine and Worcestershire sauce. Cover and cook on **Low** for 8 to 10 hours, until juices run clear when chicken is pierced with a fork.
4. Gently remove chicken from slow cooker and transfer to a platter. Cover with foil to keep warm. If desired, brown chicken under preheated broiler for 5 to 7 minutes.

5. Gravy: Pour 1 cup (250 mL) juices from slow cooker into a glass measure; skim any fat from surface. In a saucepan melt butter over medium-high heat. Add flour and cook, stirring, for 1 minute. Add measured juices and bring mixture to a boil; cook, stirring, until sauce is smooth and thickened. Season to taste with salt and pepper. Serve gravy over chicken.

Chicken in Honey-Mustard Sauce

Serves 4

For a larger crowd, you can double the chicken in this recipe and – of course – the sauce for drizzling over it.

TIP

If your liquid honey has crystallized or if, like me, you use solid creamed honey, place the jar (or as much as you need in a small bowl) in a saucepan of hot water, heating gently until melted. Or heat in microwave until melted.

When measuring honey, rub measuring cup with a little vegetable oil, then measure honey. It will easily pour out, with no sticky mess!

Cooking times for poultry may be longer for larger slow cookers and/or where there is a relatively high proportion of dark to white meat. For predominantly white-meat dishes, be sure to avoid overcooking.

MENU SUGGESTION

CHICKEN IN HONEY-MUSTARD
  SAUCE
Cooked Rice
Baked Acorn Squash
Cherry Pie

1/4 cup	butter *or* margarine	50 mL
1/2 cup	liquid honey	125 mL
1/4 cup	Dijon mustard	50 mL
1 tbsp	curry powder	15 mL
1 tsp	salt	5 mL
8	chicken pieces (legs and breasts), skin removed, if desired	8

1. In a small saucepan over medium heat (or in a small glass bowl in the microwave), melt butter. Add honey, mustard, curry powder and salt; stir until dissolved.

2. Place chicken in slow cooker. Pour honey-mustard sauce over top. Cover and cook on **Low** for 6 to 8 hours, until juices run clear when chicken is pierced with a fork. Skim off any fat from sauce and serve drizzled over chicken.

Lemony Herbed Drumsticks

Serves 4 to 6

3 to 4 lbs	chicken drumsticks	1.5 to 2 kg
1/4 cup	lemon juice	50 mL
1 cup	apple juice *or* dry white wine	250 mL
1 tbsp	olive oil	15 mL
1	onion, finely chopped	1
2	cloves garlic, minced	2
1 tsp	dried rosemary, crushed	5 mL
1/2 tsp	salt	2 mL
1/4 tsp	black pepper	1 mL

1. In a large bowl or plastic bag, place chicken, lemon juice, apple juice, olive oil, onion, garlic, rosemary, salt and pepper. Marinate 4 to 6 hours or overnight in refrigerator.

2. Transfer chicken and marinade to slow cooker. Cover and cook on **Low** for 6 to 8 hours, until chicken is lightly browned and juices run clear when pierced with a fork.

Mother Hubbard's Favorite Shepherd's Pie

Serves 6

Here's a different kind of shepherd's pie – ground chicken and vegetables topped with a buttery yellow squash topping.

To make squash purée.
Halve a 3-lb (1.5 kg) Hubbard, acorn or butternut squash, then scoop out seeds and pith. Place flesh-side down on microwave-safe plate and cover with plastic wrap. Microwave on **High** for 8 to 12 minutes or until tender. Or place in a roasting pan, flesh-side up. Pour in enough water to come 1 inch (2.5 cm) up sides of pan. Bake in a 400° F (200° C) oven for 30 to 60 minutes. Let cool. Scoop out flesh and purée in a food processor or mash well with a potato masher. Add 1 tbsp (15 mL) brown sugar and 2 tbsp (25 mL) butter or margarine to purée, mixing well.

NIGHT BEFORE

This pie can be assembled the night before. Follow preparation directions and refrigerate overnight in slow cooker stoneware. The next day, place stoneware in liner and continue cooking as directed.

1 tbsp	vegetable oil	15 mL
2 lbs	lean ground chicken	1 kg
2	onions, finely chopped	2
2	cloves garlic, minced	2
1	carrot, peeled and grated	1
1 cup	frozen corn kernels	250 mL
2/3 cup	tomato paste	150 mL
3/4 cup	water	175 mL
2 tbsp	dried parsley or (1/4 cup [50 mL] fresh)	25 mL
2 tsp	Worcestershire sauce	10 mL
1 tsp	dried thyme	5 mL
1 tsp	paprika	5 mL
1 tsp	salt	5 mL
1/2 tsp	black pepper	2 mL
4 cups	puréed Hubbard squash (see note, at left)	1 L

1. In a large nonstick skillet, heat oil over medium heat. Add ground chicken and cook, breaking up with a spoon.

2. Add onions, garlic, carrot and corn; cook 5 minutes or until vegetables are tender. Stir in tomato paste, water, parsley, Worcestershire sauce, thyme, paprika, salt and pepper, mixing well. Transfer mixture to slow cooker and cover with squash purée.

3. Cover and cook on **Low** for 6 to 8 hours or on **High** for 3 to 4 hours, until bubbling and heated through.

Plum-Good Chicken

Serves 4

Don't think that plums are only good for pies. They're also great with chicken.

TIP

TIP

It used to be that cider vinegar was the only type you could get. Now there are many varieties to choose from. Here we use rice wine vinegar – a light, low-acid, slightly sweet variety from Japan, which goes particularly well in oriental dishes. White wine vinegar (and herb vinegars, such as tarragon) also add a delightful flavor to chicken.

Cooking times for poultry may be longer for larger slow cookers and/or where there is a relatively high proportion of dark to white meat. For predominantly white-meat dishes, be sure to avoid overcooking.

VARIATION

Peachy-Good Chicken: Prepare recipe as directed but substitute canned sliced or halved peaches for the plums.

MENU SUGGESTION

PLUM-GOOD CHICKEN
Buttered Egg Noodles
Green Peas
Apple Pie à la Mode

1/4 cup	all-purpose flour	50 mL
1/2 tsp	paprika	2 mL
1/2 tsp	salt	2 mL
1/4 tsp	black pepper	1 mL
Pinch	cayenne	Pinch
8	chicken pieces (breasts or thighs), skin removed, if desired	8
1	can (14 oz [398 mL]) purple plums	1
1 tsp	ground ginger	5 mL
2 tbsp	soya sauce	25 mL
2 tbsp	rice vinegar *or* white wine vinegar	25 mL
1 tbsp	brown sugar	15 mL
2 tbsp	cornstarch	25 mL
2 tbsp	water	25 mL
1/2 tsp	cinnamon	2 mL

1. In a shallow dish or plastic bag, combine flour, paprika, salt, pepper and cayenne. Toss chicken in flour mixture to coat on all sides. Place in slow cooker.

2. Drain plums (reserving juice) and chop, discarding pits. Add to slow cooker. In a bowl combine reserved plum juice, ginger, soya sauce, vinegar and brown sugar, mixing well. Pour over chicken and plums in slow cooker.

3. Cover and cook on **Low** for 6 to 8 hours, until juices run clear when chicken is pierced with a fork.

4. In a small bowl, combine cornstarch, water and cinnamon, stirring until smooth. Add to slow cooker, cover and cook on **High** for 20 to 25 minutes or until sauce has thickened.

Polynesian Chicken

Serves 4

I love anything that reminds me of the tropics – especially in the middle of winter!

TIP

Serve over scented rice.

Instead of snow peas, try substituting broccoli florets – either way, the green adds wonderful color to this all-in-one meal.

To toast almonds: spread on a baking sheet and bake in a 350° F (180° C) oven for 5 to 7 minutes or until golden brown and fragrant.

Cooking times for poultry may be longer for larger slow cookers and/or where there is a relatively high proportion of dark to white meat. For predominantly white-meat dishes, be sure to avoid overcooking.

MAKE AHEAD

To speed up the preparation time, cook the rice in advance and refrigerate or freeze. To reheat, add 1 to 2 tbsp (15 to 25 mL) water or chicken stock and reheat in foil packets in the oven or in a covered microwave-safe dish.

1/4 cup	all-purpose flour	50 mL
1 tsp	curry powder	5 mL
1 tsp	dry mustard	5 mL
1/2 tsp	salt	2 mL
1/4 tsp	black pepper	1 mL
8	chicken thighs, skin removed if desired	8
1	can (19 oz [540 mL]) pineapple pieces, drained, juice reserved	1
4	green onions, chopped	4
1/4 cup	soya sauce	50 mL
2 tbsp	dry sherry	25 mL
1 tbsp	brown sugar	15 mL
2 tbsp	cornstarch	25 mL
1 1/2 cups	snow peas, cut in half diagonally	375 mL
	Slivered almonds, toasted	

1. In a bowl or plastic bag, combine flour, curry powder, 1/2 tsp (2 mL) of the mustard, salt and black pepper. Coat chicken in flour mixture and place in slow cooker. Add pineapple.

2. In a bowl combine all but 2 tbsp (25 mL) reserved pineapple juice, soya sauce, sherry, brown sugar and remaining 1/2 tsp (2 mL) dry mustard; stir to mix well. Pour over chicken in slow cooker.

3. Cover and cook on **Low** for 6 to 8 hours, until juices run clear when chicken is pierced with a fork.

4. In a bowl combine cornstarch and remaining pineapple juice; mix well. Pour into slow cooker. Add snow peas. Cover and cook on **High** for 15 to 20 minutes or until sauce has thickened. Serve garnished with slivered almonds.

Savory Orange Turkey Breast

Serves 4 to 6

This is simple but tasty dish brings out the best in fresh turkey breast, which is widely sold as a separate cut in supermarkets.

TIP

If you prefer dark meat, replace the turkey breast with two turkey thighs.

Look for turkey parts after a long holiday weekend, when they can be purchased more economically. Freeze them to have on hand for dishes like this one, or for other recipes.

Cooking times for poultry may be longer for larger slow cookers and/or where there is a relatively high proportion of dark to white meat. For predominantly white-meat dishes, be sure to avoid overcooking.

MENU SUGGESTION

SAVORY ORANGE TURKEY BREAST
Boiled New Potatoes
Steamed Asparagus Spears
Lemon Meringue Pie

1	bone-in turkey breast (2 to 3 lbs [1 to 1.5 kg])	1
1/2 tsp	dried thyme	2 mL
	Salt and black pepper	
1 cup	orange juice	250 mL
1	bay leaf	1

1. Season turkey breast with thyme and salt and pepper to taste. Place in slow cooker. Add orange juice and bay leaf.
2. Cover and cook on **Low** for 6 to 8 hours, until turkey is tender and no longer pink inside. Remove bay leaf and discard before carving.

Turkey Mushroom Loaf

Serves 4 to 6

VARIATION

To make a fancier version of the sauce in Step 4, sauté 1 cup (250 mL) finely chopped mushrooms in 1 tbsp (15 mL) of butter until juices have evaporated; add remaining soup and water as directed and bring to a boil. Stir in 1 tbsp (15 mL) madeira wine and a pinch of thyme.

☾ NIGHT BEFORE

Loaf can be assembled 12 hours in advance. Prepare the ingredients in the slow cooker up to the cooking stage and refrigerate in stoneware insert overnight. The next day, place stoneware in slow cooker and cook as directed.

MENU SUGGESTION

Turkey Mushroom Loaf
Mashed Potatoes
Steamed Broccoli
Baby Carrots
Pickled Beets

SLOW COOKER STONEWARE INSERT, LIGHTLY GREASED

1 1/2 lbs	ground turkey	750 g
1	can (10 oz [284 mL]) cream of mushroom soup	1
1/3 cup	fine dry breadcrumbs	75 mL
1	egg, lightly beaten	1
2	green onions, finely chopped	2
1/2 cup	finely chopped mushrooms	125 mL
1 tbsp	Worcestershire sauce	15 mL
1 tsp	dry mustard	5 mL
1/4 tsp	black pepper	1 mL
Dash	hot pepper sauce	Dash

TOPPING

2 tbsp	dry breadcrumbs	25 mL
1 tbsp	chopped fresh parsley (or 1 tsp [5 mL] dried)	15 mL

1. Fold a 2-foot (60 cm) piece of aluminum foil in half lengthwise twice, and place on bottom and up the sides of slow cooker liner.

2. In a large bowl, combine turkey, half of the soup (remainder will be used for sauce in Step 4), breadcrumbs, egg, onions, mushrooms, Worcestershire sauce, dry mustard, pepper and hot pepper sauce; mix well. Press into prepared slow cooker.

3. Topping: In a bowl combine breadcrumbs and parsley. Sprinkle over loaf. Cover and cook on **Low** for 8 to 10 hours or on **High** for 4 to 6 hours. Let stand for 15 minutes before serving.

4. Heat remaining soup with 1/4 cup (50 mL) water and serve alongside loaf.

Thai Chicken Thighs

Serves 4

8	chicken thighs (about 2 lbs [1 kg]), skin removed	8
1/2 cup	chicken stock	125 mL
1/4 cup	peanut butter	50 mL
1/4 cup	soya sauce	50 mL
2 tbsp	chopped fresh cilantro	25 mL
2 tbsp	lime juice	25 mL
1	hot chili pepper, seeded and finely chopped *or* 1/2 tsp (2 mL) cayenne pepper	1
2 tsp	minced fresh ginger root (or 1 tsp [5 mL] ground ginger)	10 mL
1/4 cup	chopped peanuts or cashews	50 mL
	Chopped fresh cilantro	

TIP

This knockout Asian dish is full of flavor. The fresh cilantro is essential – its distinctive flavor really enhances the chicken.

To store fresh ginger root, peel and place in a jar. Pour over white wine to cover. Use the infused wine to flavor other chicken dishes.

This recipe can easily be doubled for a larger crowd. Commercially prepared smooth peanut butter is fine for this sauce. But if you want more peanut flavor (and less sugar), use an all-natural peanut butter.

NIGHT BEFORE

This dish can be assembled up to 12 hours in advance. Follow preparation directions (but without adding the chopped peanuts) and refrigerate overnight in slow cooker stoneware. The next day, place stoneware in slow cooker and cook as directed.

MENU SUGGESTION

THAI CHICKEN THIGHS
Chinese Noodles
Steamed Snow Peas
Mango Sorbet

1. Place chicken thighs in slow cooker. In a bowl combine stock, peanut butter, soya sauce, cilantro, lime juice, chili pepper and ginger. Mix well and pour sauce over chicken.
2. Cover and cook on **Low** for 6 to 8 hours, until juices run clear when chicken is pierced with a fork.
3. Serve garnished with chopped peanuts and additional fresh cilantro.

Note: Cooking times for poultry may be longer for larger slow cookers and/or where there is a relatively high proportion of dark to white meat. For predominantly white-meat dishes, be sure to avoid overcooking.

Chicken Stew with Rosemary Dumplings

Serves 4 to 6

Here's the ultimate comfort food – perfect for the entire family to enjoy while gathered at the kitchen table.

TIP

This all-in-one meal works especially well in a large slow cooker since it provides plenty of room for the dumplings to cook.

To save some time, make the dumplings with 2 cups (500 mL) prepared biscuit mix combined with 1/2 tsp (2 mL) crumbled dried rosemary. Add in 3/4 cup (175 mL) milk and stir until lumpy. Continue with recipe as directed.

For fluffier dumplings, drop the dough on the chicken pieces rather than into the liquid. This will ensure that the dumplings are steamed and don't become soggy from the liquid. Also, for proper steaming, be sure the stew is piping hot.

Cooking times for poultry may be longer for larger slow cookers and/or where there is a relatively high proportion of dark to white meat. For predominantly white-meat dishes, be sure to avoid overcooking.

1/2 cup	all-purpose flour	125 mL
1 tsp	salt	5 mL
1/2 tsp	black pepper	2 mL
1	whole chicken (about 3 lbs [1.5 kg]), cut into pieces	1
1 tbsp	vegetable oil	15 mL
4	large carrots, peeled and sliced 1 inch (2.5 cm) thick	4
2	stalks celery, sliced 1/2 inch (1 cm) thick	2
1	onion, thinly sliced	1
1 tsp	dried rosemary	5 mL
2 cups	chicken stock	500 mL
1 cup	frozen peas	250 mL

DUMPLINGS

1 cup	all-purpose flour	250 mL
2 tsp	baking powder	10 mL
1/2 tsp	dried rosemary	2 mL
1/2 tsp	salt	2 mL
1/2 cup	milk	125 mL
1	egg, lightly beaten	1
	Fresh rosemary sprigs	

1. In a bowl or plastic bag, combine flour, salt and pepper. In batches, add chicken pieces to flour mixture and toss to coat. Transfer to a plate. In a large nonstick skillet, heat oil over medium-high heat. Add chicken pieces and cook for 8 to 10 minutes or until brown on all sides. Set aside.

148

NIGHT BEFORE

This stew can be assembled 12 to 24 hours in advance. Prepare stew as directed (but without adding peas and dumplings) and refrigerate in slow cooker stoneware. The next day, place stoneware in slow cooker and cook as directed.

2. Add carrots, celery, onion and rosemary to slow cooker. Set chicken pieces over vegetables. Pour 1/2 cup (125 mL) stock into skillet and cook over medium high heat, scraping up brown bits from bottom of pan. Pour pan juices into slow cooker along with remaining stock. Cover and cook on **Low** for 8 to 10 hours or on **High** for 4 to 6 hours, until vegetables are tender and stew is bubbling. Add peas and stir gently to combine.

3. Dumplings: In a bowl sift together flour, baking powder, rosemary and salt. In a measuring cup combine milk and egg. Mix well and add to flour mixture. Stir with a fork to make a lumpy dough (do not overmix – lumps are fine). Drop dumpling mixture over chicken pieces. Cover and cook on **High** for 25 to 30 minutes or until tester inserted in center of dumpling comes out clean. Serve garnished with fresh rosemary sprigs.

Tuscan Chicken Legs

Serves 8

A spicy tomato sauce enhances this Italian-inspired recipe.

Add lots of pepper and serve it with a hearty Italian red wine.

TIP

Sun-dried tomatoes can be purchased dry-packed in cellophane or oil-packed in jars. They add a rich tomato taste and texture to many dishes. If you want to cut back on the fat, you can use dry-packed tomatoes but you'll need to reconstitute them first. Simply soak in hot water for 20 minutes, then drain.

Cooking times for poultry may be longer for larger slow cookers and/or where there is a relatively high proportion of dark to white meat. For predominantly white-meat dishes, be sure to avoid overcooking.

MENU SUGGESTION

TUSCAN CHICKEN LEGS
Buttered Noodles
Steamed Broccoli
Cappuccino Ice Cream

1/4 cup	all-purpose flour	50 mL
1/2 tsp	salt	2 mL
1/4 tsp	black pepper	1 mL
8	chicken legs, separated into thigh, and drumsticks, skin removed if desired	8
2	red onions, sliced	2
6	cloves garlic, halved	6
1	can (19 oz [540 mL]) tomatoes, chopped, with juice	1
1	can (2 oz [56 g]) anchovy fillets, drained and chopped	1
3 tbsp	chopped sun-dried tomatoes (see Tip, at left)	45 mL
2 tbsp	balsamic vinegar	25 mL
2 tsp	dried Italian seasoning	10 mL
1/3 cup	drained capers	75 mL
1/2 cup	pitted black olives	125 mL

1. In a bowl or plastic bag, combine flour, salt and pepper. In batches, add chicken to flour mixture and toss to coat. Place in slow cooker. Add onions, garlic, tomatoes (with juice), anchovies, sun-dried tomatoes, vinegar and Italian seasoning.

2. Cover and cook on **Low** for 6 to 8 hours, until juices run clear when chicken is pierced with a fork.

3. Add capers and olives; cover and cook on **High** for 10 to 15 minutes before serving.

Turkey Vegetable Stew with Biscuits

Serves 4 to 6

Vegetables, turkey and biscuits combine here to make a hearty, flavorful stew.

TIP

If small new potatoes are not available, use regular-sized potatoes and cut into 2-inch (5 cm) chunks.

While homemade stock is the most flavorful, not everyone has time to make it. The next best choice is canned; use 1 can (10 oz [284 mL]) broth plus 1 can water. Avoid using bouillon cubes which have less flavor and a lot more salt.

To debone turkey thighs: Place the thigh, skin-side down, on a cutting board. With a sharp knife, cut down to the bone, then along the full length of the bone. To free the ends, slip the knife under the bone, halfway down its length. Cut away from the hand, freeing one end on the bone from the flesh. Turn the thigh around, lift the free end on the bone with one hand and cut the other end free.

2	boneless skinless turkey thighs *or* 2 lbs (1 kg) turkey breast, cut into 1-inch (2.5 cm) cubes	2
6	small new potatoes, scrubbed	6
4	carrots, peeled and chopped	4
3	stalks celery, chopped	3
2	onions, sliced	2
1 1/2 cups	chopped peeled rutabaga	375 mL
1/4 cup	all-purpose flour	50 mL
2 cups	chicken stock	500 mL
2 tbsp	tomato paste	25 mL
1 tsp	dried marjoram	5 mL
1 tsp	salt	5 mL
1/4 tsp	black pepper	1 mL
1	bay leaf	1
2 cups	prepared biscuit mix	500 mL
3/4 cup	milk	175 mL

1. Place turkey, potatoes, carrots, celery, onions and rutabaga in slow cooker. Sprinkle with flour and stir to mix. In a bowl combine stock, tomato paste, marjoram, salt and pepper; pour mixture into slow cooker. Stir to combine ingredients; add bay leaf.

2. Cover and cook on **Low** for 6 to 8 hours or on **High** for 4 to 6 hours, until vegetables are tender and stew is bubbling. Remove bay leaf and discard.

3. In a bowl combine biscuit mix and milk. Stir with a fork to make a lumpy dough (do not overmix – lumps are fine). Drop spoonfuls of dough over hot stew. Cover and cook on **High** for 20 to 25 minutes or until tester inserted in center of dumpling comes out clean.

Note: Cooking times for poultry may be longer for larger slow cookers and/or where there is a relatively high proportion of dark to white meat. For predominantly white-meat dishes, be sure to avoid overcooking.

Party-Style Chicken and Sausage Stew

Serves 8

1 lb	hot Italian sausage	500 g
1/4 cup	all-purpose flour	50 mL
1/2 tsp	salt	2 mL
1/4 tsp	black pepper	1 mL
3 to 4 lbs	chicken legs, separated into thighs and drumsticks, skin removed if desired	1.5 to 2 kg
4	carrots, peeled and chopped	4
2	onions, sliced	2
3	large cloves garlic, halved	3
1	can (28 oz [796 mL]) plum tomatoes, drained and quartered	1
1/2 cup	chicken stock	125 mL
2 tsp	Italian seasoning	10 mL
1 tsp	dry mustard	5 mL
1	yellow pepper, cut into strips	1
1	red bell pepper, cut into strips	1
2	small zucchini, sliced	2

TIP

This dish is the perfect dish to serve when you have a house full of guests and don't want to spend a lot of time in the kitchen. For this quantity, a large (6-quart) slow cooker is best. If you have a smaller slow cooker (or fewer mouths to feed) simply cut the recipe in half.

Cooking times for poultry may be longer for larger slow cookers and/or where there is a relatively high proportion of dark to white meat. For predominantly white-meat dishes, be sure to avoid overcooking.

NIGHT BEFORE

This dish can be assembled the night before. Follow preparation directions (but without adding peppers and zucchini) and refrigerate overnight in slow cooker stoneware. The next day, place stoneware in slow cooker and continue cooking as directed.

MENU SUGGESTION

Hot Buttered Rum (see recipe, page 33)
Party-Style Chicken and Sausage Stew

1. In a large nonstick skillet over medium-high heat, cook sausages for 6 to 8 minutes or until brown on all sides. Slice into 1-inch (2.5 cm) pieces and transfer to slow cooker.

2. In a bowl or plastic bag, combine flour, salt and pepper. In batches, add chicken to flour mixture and toss to coat. Transfer chicken to slow cooker Add carrots, onions, garlic and tomatoes.

3. In a bowl combine stock, Italian seasoning and dry mustard; stir to mix. Pour into slow cooker.

4. Cover and cook on **Low** for 6 to 8 hours, until carrots are tender and stew is bubbling. Add yellow pepper, red pepper and zucchini. Cover and cook on **High** for another 15 to 20 minutes before serving.

Grains & Vegetables

Caramelized Onion and Apple Bake

Serves 4 to 6

2 tbsp	butter *or* margarine	25 mL
4	large onions, sliced	4
1 tbsp	granulated sugar	15 mL
8 oz	sliced mushrooms	250 g
1	Granny Smith apple, peeled, cored and finely chopped	1
2 tbsp	all-purpose flour	25 mL
3/4 cup	chicken stock	175 mL
1/4 cup	light cream cheese, softened	50 mL
2 tbsp	dry sherry	25 mL
1/2 tsp	salt	2 mL
1/4 tsp	black pepper	1 mL
1/2 cup	toasted sliced almonds	125 mL
1/4 tsp	paprika	1 mL

If you like creamed onions, you'll absolutely love this luxurious dish. The secret of its extra-rich color and flavor comes from caramelizing the onions.

TIP

Serve this side dish with succulent roasted chicken or turkey, or a spectacular prime rib.

Tearless onions. Why is it that the doorbell always rings when you've got tears streaming down your face from slicing onions? To avoid this problem, put onions in the freezer for a few minutes before chopping.

1. In a large skillet, melt butter over medium heat. Add onions and sugar. Cover and cook, stirring occasionally, for 12 to 15 minutes or until onions are softened and nicely colored. With a slotted spoon, remove from skillet and set aside.

2. To same skillet add mushrooms and apple and an additional tablespoon (15 mL) of butter if necessary. Cook, stirring, for 6 to 8 minutes or until mushrooms have softened and released their liquid. Blend in flour and then stock. Bring mixture to a boil and cook, stirring constantly, until slightly thickened. Stir in cream cheese until melted. Remove from heat. Stir in sherry, salt, pepper and reserved onions.

To toast almonds: Spread onto a baking sheet and bake in a 350° F (180° C) oven, stirring once or twice, for 7 to 8 minutes, or until lightly brown and fragrant. Remove from heat and allow to cool completely.

3. Transfer onion mixture to prepared slow cooker and sprinkle with toasted almonds and paprika. Cover and cook on **Low** for 6 to 8 hours or on **High** for 3 to 4 hours, until set and heated through.

Tangy Red Cabbage with Apples

Serves 6

This is a great side dish for any meal, especially a chicken, pork or sausage entrée.

TIP

Don't worry about being too precise with the cooking time in this recipe – the cabbage can steam away on **Low** all day.

If you are using a food processor to shred the cabbage, use it also for the onions and apples; it will save you a lot of time.

Leftover cabbage can be frozen until needed. Pack in freezer-safe containers and store for up to 3 months. To reheat, microwave on **High** until hot.

Adjust the sugar and vinegar to suit your taste.

The vinegar not only adds flavor, but helps preserve the red color of the cabbage.

3 lbs	red cabbage, shredded (about 10 cups [2.5 L])	1.5 kg
2	Granny Smith apples, peeled, cored and thinly sliced	2
1	onion, sliced	1
1/4 cup	red wine vinegar	50 mL
1/4 cup	packed brown sugar	50 mL
2 tbsp	butter *or* margarine	25 mL
1/2 cup	water	125 mL
1 tsp	salt	5 mL
1 tsp	celery seed	5 mL
1/2 tsp	black pepper	2 mL

1. In slow cooker, toss together cabbage, apples and onion slices.
2. In a saucepan over medium-high heat, combine vinegar, brown sugar, butter, water, salt, celery seed and pepper. Bring mixture to a boil, reduce heat and simmer for 1 minute or until butter is melted and sugar is dissolved. Pour over cabbage mixture in slow cooker.
3. Cover and cook on **Low** for 4 to 6 hours or until cabbage is tender.

Root Vegetables in Balsamic Vinegar

Serves 4 to 6

I love the way slow braising brings out the sweet flavors of the hearty winter vegetables in this dish. It's a wonderful accompaniment to a Sunday night roast.

TIP

The finest balsamic vinegar comes from Italy, where it is aged for years in wooden barrels. Its sweet-and-sour flavor and rich, winey aroma make it superb as a salad dressing, or as a splash in hearty soups and stews. In fact, "vintage" balsamic vinegar is often more expensive than wine – and Italians drink it as an after-dinner *digestif*.

4 to 6	medium potatoes, peeled and cut in 2-inch [5 cm] chunks	4 to 6
3	large carrots, peeled and chopped	3
2	large parsnips, peeled and chopped	2
2	medium onions, quartered	2
1 cup	vegetable or chicken stock	250 mL
1/4 cup	balsamic vinegar	50 mL
2 tbsp	brown sugar	25 mL
1/2 tsp	salt	2 mL
1/4 tsp	black pepper	1 mL

1. In slow cooker, combine potatoes, carrots, parsnips and onions.
2. In a bowl combine stock, vinegar, sugar, salt and pepper; mix well. Pour over vegetables in slow cooker.
3. Cover and cook, stirring once every hour, on **Low** for 8 to 10 hours or on **High** for 4 to 6 hours, until vegetables are tender.

Cheddar Scalloped Potatoes

Serves 6

This has got to be everyone's favorite potato dish. It goes well with ham, pork, chicken or turkey. My friend (and die-hard potato lover) Kathy Shortt was my principal taste-tester for this recipe. She gave it a perfect 10!

MAKE AHEAD

This dish can be prepared a day ahead. Combine liquid ingredients and pour over potato and onion slices. Cover and refrigerate up to 24 hours. Bake as directed.

TIP

If you don't have a blender or food processor, finely chop all ingredients for the milk sauce. Pour over potatoes and continue as directed.

6	medium potatoes, peeled and sliced	6
1	medium onion, sliced	1
1/4 cup	celery leaves	50 mL
1 tbsp	dried parsley	15 mL
2 tbsp	butter or margarine, melted	25 mL
1/4 cup	all-purpose flour	50 mL
1 tsp	salt	5 mL
1/2 tsp	black pepper	2 mL
1	can (13 oz [385 mL]) evaporated milk	1
1 cup	grated Cheddar cheese	250 mL
1/2 tsp	paprika	2 mL

1. Layer potato slices and onion in prepared slow cooker.

2. In a blender or food processor, combine celery leaves, parsley, butter, flour, salt, pepper, evaporated milk and Cheddar cheese. Process for 1 minute or until mixture is smooth. Pour over potatoes and onions; sprinkle with paprika.

3. Cover and cook on **Low** for 6 to 8 hours or on **High** for 3 to 4 hours, until potatoes are tender and heated through.

Honey-Orange Braised Carrots

Serves 4

This dish is a wonderful choice to accompany holiday roast turkey or beef. To save time, use packages of whole, peeled, baby carrots.

TIP

You can double the quantity of carrots in this the recipe, but only increase the sauce ingredients by half since there is very little evaporation in slow cooking.

To get the most juice out of an orange, roll on the countertop, pressing down with the palm of your hand, or microwave at **High** for 20 seconds before squeezing. One orange should yield about 1/2 cup (125 mL) squeezed juice.

1 lb	peeled baby carrots	500 g
1/2 cup	freshly squeezed orange juice	125 mL
2 tbsp	liquid honey	25mL
1 tbsp	melted butter or margarine	15 mL
1 tsp	ground ginger	5 mL
1/2 tsp	orange zest	2 mL
1 tbsp	chopped fresh parsley	15 mL
	Salt and black pepper to taste	

1. Place carrots in a slow cooker. In a 2-cup (500 mL) glass measure or bowl, combine orange juice, honey, butter, ginger and orange zest. Pour over carrots.

2. Cover and cook, stirring once, on **Low** for 6 to 8 hours or on **High** for 3 to 4 hours, until carrots are nicely glazed. Serve sprinkled with parsley and seasoned to taste with salt and pepper.

Mashed Potato Soufflé

Serves 6

SLOW COOKER STONEWARE INSERT, LIGHTLY BUTTERED

While not a true soufflé, this dish has the same kind of light texture and is great to serve alongside roast turkey or beef. And because it's prepared in the slow cooker, it also helps to free up valuable oven space when there are plenty of other side dishes to keep warm.

TIP

The fluffiness of your mash depends on the type of potatoes used. The creamy-yellow Yukon Gold variety has a wonderful buttery flavor and makes a delicious mashed potato. Russet potatoes also work very well. Regular white potatoes, while not as flavorful, also mash well. In fact, the only type that really don't work are new potatoes, since they don't have a very high starch content.

10 to 12	potatoes, scrubbed, peeled and cut into chunks	10 to 12
1/3 cup	butter	75 mL
1	pkg (8 oz [250 g]) light or regular cream cheese, softened	1
1 cup	light or regular sour cream	250 mL
2	eggs, separated	2
1 tsp	salt	5 mL
1/2 tsp	black pepper	2 mL
1/4 cup	fine dry breadcrumbs	50 mL

1. In a large saucepan of boiling, salted water, cook potatoes for 20 minutes or until fork tender. Drain well and return to saucepan. Add 1/4 cup (50 mL) of the butter, cream cheese, sour cream, egg yolks, salt and pepper.

2. Mash potatoes with a potato masher or with an electric mixer at low speed until smooth. (Do not use a food processor or potatoes will end up with a glue-like consistency.) In another bowl, beat egg whites until stiff but not dry. Fold into potato mixture. Spoon into prepared slow cooker.

3. In a small bowl, combine remaining 2 tbsp (25 mL) butter and breadcrumbs; mix well and sprinkle over potatoes. (Mixture can be prepared up to this point and refrigerated for 24 hours.)

4. Cover and cook on **High** for 3 to 4 hours or until puffy and slightly brown on top. Serve immediately.

BAKED LEMON SPONGE (PAGE 169) ➤

Pecan Mushroom Wild Rice

Serves 6 to 8

2 tbsp	butter *or* margarine	25 mL
1	onion, finely chopped	1
8 oz	sliced mushrooms	250 g
1/2 cup	chopped pecans or almonds	125 mL
1 cup	wild rice	250 mL
2 cups	chicken stock	500 mL

1. In a large skillet, melt butter over medium-high heat. Add onion, mushrooms and pecans; sauté for 7 to 8 minutes or until vegetables are tender and nuts are fragrant. Add rice and cook for another 3 minutes. Transfer mixture to slow cooker and pour in stock.
2. Cover and cook on **Low** for 6 to 8 hours or on **High** for 2 to 3 hours, until most of the liquid has been absorbed. Fluff with a fork before serving.

≺ RHUBARB-BLUEBERRY PUDDING CAKE (PAGE 178)

Rich Spinach Casserole

Serves 4 to 6

This casserole is a wonderful companion to any grilled meat. Use it as an alternative to potatoes.

TIP

Always choose spinach that has crisp, bright leaves and a light, fresh aroma. (If it smells like cabbage, it's too old.) Wash well, then trim the stems before using in recipes or salads.

As a time-saving alternative to fresh spinach in this recipe, substitute 3 packages (each 10 oz [300 g]) frozen chopped spinach, thawed and squeezed dry.

Spinach can be washed, dried and torn, then wrapped loosely in paper towels and refrigerated in a sealed plastic bag for up to 2 days.

2 lbs	fresh spinach leaves *or* 2 packages (each 10 oz [300 g]) spinach, washed, tough stems removed	1 kg
1 cup	light or regular cottage cheese	250 mL
1/4 cup	light sour cream	50 mL
3	eggs, lightly beaten	3
2 tbsp	all-purpose flour	25 mL
1/2 tsp	ground nutmeg	2 mL
1/2 tsp	salt	2 mL
1	can (10 oz [284 mL]) water chestnuts, drained and finely chopped	1

1. Place spinach in a large pot of boiling, salted water. Cook over high heat, stirring, just until wilted. Place spinach in a colander to drain. Squeeze out moisture by hand; wrap in a clean, dry towel and squeeze out additional moisture. Once cooled, coarsely chop spinach.

2. In a bowl combine cottage cheese, sour cream, eggs, flour, nutmeg and salt; mix well. Stir in chopped spinach and water chestnuts. Transfer mixture to prepared slow cooker.

3. Cover and cook on **Low** for 4 to 6 hours or on **High** for 2 to 3 hours, until casserole is set.

Sweet Potato Custard

Serves 6

This side dish is the perfect companion to turkey, ham or roast pork. Try it with your next Thanksgiving or Easter meal.

VARIATION

Carrot Custard: Substitute 6 cups (1. 5 L) peeled and chopped carrots for the sweet potatoes.

5 cups	chopped peeled sweet potatoes	1.25 L
2 tsp	lemon juice	10 mL
2 tbsp	softened butter	25 mL
1/4 cup	packed brown sugar	50 mL
1 tsp	salt	5 mL
1/2 tsp	paprika	2 mL
1	egg	1
1/4 cup	light or regular sour cream	50 mL

1. In a pot of boiling water, cook sweet potatoes for 15 to 20 minutes or until tender. Drain and transfer to a blender or food processor. Purée or mash sweet potatoes until smooth. Add lemon juice.

2. In a bowl combine butter, brown sugar, salt, paprika, egg and sour cream; beat until smooth. Fold in potato purée and transfer to prepared slow cooker.

3. Cover and cook on **Low** for 4 to 6 hours or on **High** for 2 to 3 hours, until custard is set and slightly browned around the edges.

Cider-Braised Turnips

Serves 4 to 6

Even if you've never been a huge fan of turnips or rutabagas, this side dish is sure to make you one. The sweet flavor of the apple cider complements the tartness of this hearty winter vegetable.

For extra sweetness, add an additional 2 tbsp (25 mL) brown sugar to the turnip and cider before cooking.

Turnips are often confused with rutabagas. Although the rutabaga is a member of the turnip family, it is large, yellow-fleshed and slightly sweeter than the turnip. In this recipe (and others), the two can be used interchangeably – and both can be stored all winter in a cold cellar. Remember to remove the waxy outer skin before cooking.

MAKE AHEAD

Turnip can be cooked in the cider a day ahead, puréed, then refrigerated until ready to use. Reheat in slow cooker on **Low** for 2 to 3 hours or until heated through.

4 cups	diced peeled turnip or rutabaga (about 2 lbs [1 kg])	1 L
2 cups	apple cider	500 mL
2 tbsp	butter *or* margarine	25 mL
2 tbsp	brown sugar	25 mL
1/4 tsp	ground nutmeg	1 mL
	Salt and black pepper to taste	

1. In slow cooker, combine turnip and cider. Cover and cook on **Low** for 8 to 10 hours or on **High** for 4 to 6 hours, until turnip is tender and most of the cider has evaporated.

2. In a bowl with a potato masher or in a food processor, mash or purée turnip. Add butter, brown sugar and nutmeg; mix well. Season to taste with salt and pepper. If not serving immediately, return mixture to slow cooker, cover and keep warm on **Low** until ready to serve.

Sweet Endings

Almond-Pear Steamed Pudding with Coconut-Lime Sauce

Serves 6 to 8

6-CUP (1.5 L) BOWL OR PUDDING MOLD, GREASED

This lovely steamed pudding combines two of my favorite ingredients – pears and toasted coconut.

TIP

If you like a smooth clear sauce, omit the coconut. However, I love the texture it adds.

For the purée, use canned pears or two very ripe, fresh pears – or use a small jar of baby food pears, which is just the right size for the amount suggested in this recipe.

You will need a large (5- to 6 1/2-quart) slow cooker so your soufflé dish or bowl will fit and can be easily removed. Be sure to use long oven mitts when lifting out the soufflé dish, so the steam doesn't burn your arms.

To toast coconut: Spread onto a baking sheet and bake in a 350° F (180° C) oven, stirring once or twice, for 7 to 8 minutes or until golden brown. Remove from heat and let cool completely.

1/4 cup	butter, softened	50 mL
3 tbsp	almond paste or marzipan, softened	45 mL
3/4 cup	granulated sugar	175 mL
1 cup	cake-and-pastry flour	250 mL
1 tsp	baking powder	5 mL
1/2 cup	toasted shredded coconut	125 mL
2	eggs	2
1/2 tsp	almond extract	2 mL
1/2 cup	puréed pears, canned or fresh (see Tip , at left)	125 mL
1	egg white	1

COCONUT-LIME SAUCE

3/4 cup	granulated sugar	175 mL
2 tbsp	cornstarch	25 mL
1 cup	water	250 mL
1/4 cup	lime juice	50 mL
1/2 cup	toasted shredded coconut	125 mL
1 tsp	grated lime zest	5 mL

1. In a large bowl, beat together butter, almond paste and 1/2 cup (125 mL) sugar until light and fluffy.

2. In a separate bowl, sift together flour and baking powder. Stir in coconut. Add eggs, almond extract and pears, mixing until smooth. Gradually stir in almond paste mixture.

3. In a small bowl, beat egg white until foamy; add remaining 2 tbsp (25 mL) sugar and beat until soft peaks form. Gently fold egg white into batter and pour batter into prepared bowl. Secure cover on pudding mold, or cover bowl with aluminum foil and secure with an elastic band. Place in slow cooker and add boiling water to reach halfway up sides of mold. Cover slow cooker and steam pudding on **High** for 4 to 5 hours (do not cook for a longer time on **Low**). Remove mold from slow cooker and allow pudding to cool. Pudding will be moist around the edges.

4. To unmold pudding, run a knife around edges to loosen. Invert onto a serving platter and carefully lift off mold. Cool to room temperature.

5. Coconut-Lime Sauce: In a saucepan over medium-high heat, combine sugar and cornstarch. Whisk in water and lime juice. Cook, stirring constantly, until mixture comes to a boil. Reduce heat and simmer, stirring constantly, until thickened. Stir in coconut and lime zest. Serve sauce over pudding.

Aunt Beatty's Betty

Serves 6

This wonderful dessert reminds me of the traditional one my Aunt Beatty, a charming English lady, used to make. Be sure to serve it warm with whipping cream, vanilla ice cream or LAZY CREAM (see recipe, page 170).

(see recipe, page 170).

TIP

To quickly soften butter, remove foil wrapping and place cold butter in microwave-safe dish. For every 1/2 cup (125 mL) butter, microwave on Defrost for 45 seconds to 1 minute.

6	large baking apples, peeled and sliced	6
2 tbsp	granulated sugar	25 mL
1 tsp	cinnamon	5 mL

TOPPING

1/2 cup	softened butter	125 mL
1 cup	lightly packed brown sugar	250 mL
3/4 cup	all-purpose flour	175 mL

1. In a large bowl, toss together apples, sugar and cinnamon. Place in slow cooker.
2. In a bowl combine butter and brown sugar. Add flour and mix together with a spoon until mixture is crumbly. Sprinkle over apples and pat firmly into a crust.
3. Cover and cook on **High** for 3 to 4 hours or until apples are tender and sauce is bubbly.

Baked Lemon Sponge

Serves 4

1 cup	granulated sugar	250 mL
1/4 cup	all-purpose flour	50 mL
1/4 tsp	salt	1 mL
1/4 cup	lemon juice	50 mL
1 tbsp	grated lemon zest	15 mL
3	eggs, separated	3
1 tbsp	melted butter	15 mL
1 cup	milk	250 mL
1 tbsp	icing sugar	15 mL

1. In a bowl combine sugar, flour and salt. Stir in lemon juice, lemon zest, egg yolks, butter and milk.

2. In another bowl, beat egg whites until stiff peaks form; fold gently into lemon mixture. Pour into pre- pared bowl and cover tightly with aluminum foil (secure with an elastic band). Place in slow cooker and pour in enough water to come 1 inch (2.5 cm) up sides of bowl.

3. Cover and cook on **High** for 2 to 3 hours or until topping is set and light and fluffy. Sift icing sugar over sponge before serving.

TIP

As this lovely old-fashioned dessert steams in the slow cooker, it separates into a cake-like topping with a creamy lemon custard sauce underneath. Sprinkle with icing sugar before serving.

While this dessert is great on its own, it's also delicious served over a mixture of fresh raspberries, strawber- ries and blueberries.

You will need to use a large (5- to 6 1/2-quart) slow cook- er so your soufflé dish or bowl will fit and can be easily removed. Be sure to use long oven mitts when lifting out the soufflé dish, so the steam doesn't burn your arms.

To get the most juice from a lemon, leave at room tempera- ture and roll on counter, press- ing down with the palm of your hand, before squeezing.

To zest a lemon, use the fine edge of a cheese grater, ensuring you don't grate the white pith underneath. Or use a zester to remove the zest, then finely chop. Zesters are inexpensive and widely available at specialty kitchen shops.

Bayou Bread Pudding with Rum Sauce and Lazy Cream

Serves 6 to 8

I was inspired to make this dish after our book club read a wonderful tale set in the steamy heart of the Bayou. This dessert is so-o-o-o-o authentically good, everyone will be saying "y'all" by the end of the evening.

TIP

To make the bread cubes: Cut the bread into 1/2-inch [1 cm] slices then cut each slice into 4 pieces. If you have the time, cut bread into cubes the night before and allow them to dry out overnight. However, if time is a factor, you can speed up the process by baking the cubes in a preheated 200° F (100° C) oven, turning once, for 20 to 30 minutes or until dry.

1/3 cup	melted butter or margarine	75 mL
16 cups	day-old French bread cubes, lightly packed (see Tip, at left)	4 L
1 cup	golden raisins	250 mL
3	eggs	3
1 1/2 cups	granulated sugar	375 mL
2 tbsp	vanilla	25 mL
1 tsp	ground nutmeg	5 mL
1 tsp	cinnamon	5 mL
3 cups	milk	750 mL

RUM SAUCE

1/2 cup	packed brown sugar	125 mL
2 tbsp	all-purpose flour	25 mL
1/4 tsp	salt	1 mL
1 cup	water	250 mL
1/2 tsp	vanilla	2 mL
2 tbsp	dark or amber rum	25 mL

LAZY CREAM

1 cup	whipping (35%) cream	250 mL
3 tbsp	icing sugar	45 mL
2 tbsp	light or regular sour cream	25 mL
1 tsp	vanilla	5 mL

1. Brush 2 tbsp (25 mL) of the melted butter on bottom and up the sides of a slow cooker stoneware insert. Layer bread cubes and raisins in slow cooker.

2. In a large bowl, beat together eggs and sugar until thickened and lemon-yellow colored. Add vanilla, nutmeg, cinnamon, milk and remaining 1/4 cup (50 mL) butter; beat for 1 minute longer to combine. Pour mixture evenly over bread, pressing down on cubes to saturate. Cover and cook on **Low** for 6 to 7 hours or on **High** for 3 to 4 hours, until golden brown and slightly puffed. Allow pudding to cool slightly before serving.

3. Rum Sauce: In a saucepan over medium-high heat, mix together sugar, flour and salt (this will avoid any lumps). Stir in water and vanilla. Bring mixture to a boil; reduce heat and simmer, stirring constantly, until mixture thickens. Stir in rum.

4. Lazy Cream: In a bowl combine whipping cream, icing sugar, sour cream and vanilla. Beat until soft peaks form (do not overbeat). Cover tightly and refrigerate until ready to serve.

5. To serve, pour warm rum sauce into bottom of serving dish. Spoon warm pudding over top and dollop with Lazy Cream.

Carrot Marmalade Pudding with Lemon Sauce

Serves 4

6-CUP (1.5 L) BOWL OR PUDDING MOLD, BUTTERED

Instead of a traditional Christmas pudding, my mother makes a carrot pudding. It's every bit as satisfying – and every bit as spectacular to watch when doused with brandy and set aflame. I love it with the citrusy lemon sauce featured here, but feel free to try it with a richer butterscotch sauce.

TIP

You will need to use a large (5- to 6 1/2-quart) slow cooker so your pudding bowl will fit and can be easily removed. Be sure to use long oven mitts when lifting out the bowl so the steam doesn't burn your arms.

If you don't have a pudding mold, a heat-proof mixing bowl works very well. Instead of a lid, use aluminum foil secured with an elastic band.

To grate lemon or orange zest, a zester tool can be purchased very inexpensively at kitchen shops. Or you can use the smallest holes on a cheese grater.

CARROT PUDDING

1 1/4 cups	grated carrots	300 mL
1 cup	fine dry breadcrumbs	250 mL
1 cup	brown sugar	250 mL
1/2 cup	chopped dates	125 mL
1/2 cup	chopped candied cherries	125 mL
1/2 cup	chopped walnuts or pecans	125 mL
1/2 cup	seedless raisins	125 mL
1/2 cup	golden raisins or currants	125 mL
1/2 cup	shortening, softened	125 mL
1/4 cup	butter, softened	50 mL
3	eggs, lightly beaten	3
1/4 cup	orange marmalade	50 mL
2 tbsp	molasses	25 mL
2 tbsp	dry sherry or white grape juice	25 mL
1 cup	all-purpose flour	250 mL
1 tsp	baking powder	5 mL
1/2 tsp	baking soda	2mL
1 tsp	salt	5 mL
1 tsp	cinnamon	5 mL
1/2 tsp	ground nutmeg	2 mL
1/2 tsp	ground allspice	2 mL
1/4 tsp	ground cloves	1 mL

LEMON SAUCE

1/2 cup	granulated sugar	125 mL
1 tbsp	cornstarch	15 mL
1 cup	boiling water	250 mL
2 tbsp	butter	25 mL
1/2 tsp	grated lemon zest	2 mL
2 tbsp	lemon juice	25 mL

1. In a bowl combine carrots, breadcrumbs, brown sugar, dates, cherries, walnuts, seedless raisins and golden raisins; stir to mix well and set aside. In a separate bowl, beat shortening and butter together until light and fluffy. Add eggs, one at a time, beating well after each addition. Add marmalade, molasses and sherry; mix well. Sift together flour, baking powder, baking soda, salt, cinnamon, nutmeg, allspice and cloves; beat into shortening mixture to form a batter. Fold fruit into batter, stirring until just combined.

2. Pour batter into prepared bowl; secure cover on pudding mold or cover bowl with aluminum foil and secure with an elastic band. Place in slow cooker and add boiling water to come 1 inch (2.5 cm) up the sides of bowl.

3. Cover slow cooker and steam on **High** for 4 1/2 to 5 hours (do not cook for a longer time on **Low**) or until a toothpick inserted in center of pudding comes out clean. Remove from slow cooker and let stand for 5 minutes.

4. To unmold, run a knife around edges of pudding to loosen. Invert onto a serving platter and carefully lift off mold. Set aside to cool.

5. Lemon Sauce: In a saucepan over low heat, mix together sugar and cornstarch. Whisk in boiling water. Cook until clear, stirring frequently. Remove from heat and stir in butter, zest and lemon juice. Serve warm over pudding.

Caramel Peaches

Serves 4 to 6

This easy-to-make dessert combines fresh juicy peaches with a sweet butterscotch sauce. It's the perfect dish to whip together when unexpected guests arrive.

TIP

Serve these peaches over vanilla ice cream or simply enjoy them on their own. You can substitute sliced apples for the peaches.

To quickly ripen fresh peaches, place in a brown paper bag and let stand overnight at room temperature.

To peel peaches, plunge in boiling water for 30 seconds to loosen skin and quickly plunge into cold water. Skin should easily slip off.

6	peaches, peeled and sliced *or* 3 cans (each 14 oz [398 mL]) peach halves, drained and sliced	6
2 tsp	lemon juice	10 mL
1 cup	packed brown sugar	250 mL
3 tbsp	melted butter or margarine	45 mL
1/4 cup	whipping (35%) cream	50 mL
1/2 tsp	cinnamon	2 mL
	Vanilla ice cream (optional)	

1. In a bowl toss together peach slices and lemon juice.
2. In slow cooker, combine brown sugar, butter, cream and cinnamon; mix well. Add peach slices and toss to coat with brown sugar mixture.
3. Cover and cook on **Low** for 4 to 6 hours. If desired, serve over vanilla ice cream.

Cranberry Apple Cobbler

Serves 8

Grab a big ol' spoon and sink into a cuddly sofa to enjoy this tangy comfort-food classic. Here, tangy cranberries are paired with sweet apples under a soft, light cake topping.

TIP

Serve this cobbler warm with ice cream or drizzle with homemade or store-bought custard sauce.

When they're in season, purchase 2 or 3 extra bags of cranberries and toss them into the freezer to have on hand anytime. There is no need to defrost before using.

1	pkg (12 oz [340 g]) cranberries, fresh or frozen	1
3/4 cup	granulated sugar	175 mL
3 tbsp	cornstarch	45 mL
1/2 tsp	cinnamon	2 mL
1 cup	cranberry juice	250 mL
8 cups	sliced peeled apples (about 6)	2 L

TOPPING

1 1/2 cups	all-purpose flour	375 mL
1/3 cup	granulated sugar	75 mL
1 tbsp	baking powder	15 mL
1/4 tsp	salt	1 mL
1/2 cup	cubed cold butter	125 mL
2/3 cup	milk	150 mL
1 tsp	granulated sugar	5 mL
1/4 tsp	cinnamon	1 mL

1. Place cranberries in bottom of slow cooker. Add sugar, cornstarch and cinnamon, tossing to coat. Add cranberry juice and apples; stir to combine. Cover and cook on **Low** for 6 to 8 hours or on **High** for 3 to 4 hours.

2. In a bowl combine flour, sugar, baking powder and salt. With a pastry blender or 2 knives, cut in butter until mixture resembles coarse crumbs. Drizzle with milk and stir with a fork until a thick batter forms.

3. Drop batter by spoonfuls over fruit mixture. Cover and cook on **High** for 30 to 45 minutes or until a toothpick inserted in the center of dumplings comes out clean. In a bowl combine sugar and cinnamon; sprinkle over dumplings before serving.

Honey-Orange Crème Caramel

Serves 6

1 cup	granulated sugar	250 mL
1/2 cup	water	125 mL

HONEY-ORANGE CUSTARD

1	can (13 oz [385 mL]) evaporated milk	1
1/4 cup	1% or 2% milk	50 mL
	Grated zest of 1 orange	
3	eggs, lightly beaten	3
1/4 cup	honey	50 mL
1 tbsp	Grand Marnier *or* orange juice	15 mL

This decadent treat will remind you of the rich dessert that you get in expensive restaurants. Slow cooking ensures a smooth, creamy custard without overbaking.

TIP

You will need to use a large (5 to 6 1/2 quart) slow cooker so your soufflé dish will fit and can be easily removed. Be sure to use long oven mitts when lifting out the soufflé dish, so the steam doesn't burn your arms.

Custard-type recipes work best in the slow cooker when they are baked in a soufflé dish placed in the stoneware insert. If cooked directly in the stoneware, the eggs in the custard will have a tendency to curdle during the long cooking process.

1. In a saucepan over medium heat, combine sugar and water. Stirring constantly with a wooden spoon, cook until sugar is dissolved and mixture comes to a boil. Stop stirring and continue to cook for 4 minutes or until golden brown. Pour into soufflé dish, tilting dish to distribute syrup evenly over bottom and up the sides. Set aside. (Alternatively, place sugar and water mixture in microwave; cover tightly with plastic wrap but leave slight space for steam to escape. Cook on **High** for 8 to 10 minutes or until golden brown.)

2. In a saucepan over medium-low heat, combine evaporated milk, milk and orange zest. Gently heat until mixture begins to simmer. Remove from heat and let stand for 10 minutes. With a fork, remove zest from saucepan and discard.

3. In a bowl combine eggs, honey and Grand Marnier. Gradually whisk in warm milk mixture. Pour into prepared soufflé dish. Cover with aluminum foil and secure with an elastic band. Place soufflé dish in slow cooker and pour in about 2 cups (500 mL) hot water.

To keep a baking dish raised off the bottom of your slow cooker, you can use a trivet or small baking rack. But I find that a collapsible vegetable steamer also works well – and it's also useful for lifting the bowl out of the slow cooker. Place steamer on the bottom of stoneware and open as much as possible. Place soufflé dish or bowl on steamer and pour in enough water to come up sides 1 inch (2.5 cm). Steam as directed.

This dessert is best made ahead so it can be chilled before serving. Make it early in the day or even a full day ahead.

4. Cover slow cooker and steam for 2 to 2 1/2 hours on **High** or until knife inserted in custard comes out clean. Remove soufflé dish from slow cooker and refrigerate for 3 to 4 hours or overnight.

5. To unmold, run a sharp knife around outside edge of custard. Dip bottom of dish in hot water for a few moments and invert onto a serving plate, giving a firm shake to release the custard and sauce.

Rhubarb-Blueberry Pudding Cake

Serves 6 to 8

Stewed blueberries and rhubarb topped with a steamed dumpling crust make a wonderful old-fashioned dessert. I like to make this with the rhubarb from my garden. I freeze it and bring out as much as I need so it's ready at hand for special recipes such as this one.

TIP

If fresh rhubarb or blueberries are unavailable, use frozen. There is no need to thaw them first.

SLOW COOKER STONEWARE INSERT, LIGHTLY GREASED

1 cup	chopped fresh or frozen rhubarb	250 mL
2 cups	fresh or frozen blueberries	500 mL
1/4 cup	butter	50 mL
1 1/4 cups	granulated sugar	300 mL
3/4 cup	all-purpose flour	75 mL
1 tsp	baking powder	5 mL
1/2 tsp	cinnamon	2 mL
1/4 tsp	ground nutmeg	1 mL
Pinch	salt	Pinch
1/2 cup	milk	125 mL
1 tbsp	cornstarch	15 mL
1 tsp	grated orange zest	5 mL
1/2 cup	orange juice	125 mL
	Whipped cream (optional)	

1. Place rhubarb and blueberries in prepared slow cooker.

2. In a bowl cream together butter and 3/4 cup (175 mL) of the granulated sugar. In another bowl combine flour, baking powder, cinnamon, nutmeg and salt. Add to butter mixture alternately with milk. Spread over fruit in slow cooker.

3. In a small saucepan, combine cornstarch and grated orange zest. Stir in orange juice. Bring orange juice to a boil over medium-high heat; cook, stirring constantly, until slightly thickened. Remove from heat and pour over batter in slow cooker.

4. Cover and cook on **High** for 2 to 3 hours or until top is golden and fruit is bubbly. Serve warm with dollops of whipped cream, if desired.

Upside-Down Fudge Brownie Pudding

Serves 4 to 6

In this wonderfully rich dessert, the fudgy batter rises to the top, leaving a delicious chocolate sauce beneath.

TIP

This dish is a must with vanilla ice cream! If you happen to have any left over, refrigerate and eat cold the next day. It's equally delicious.

To grease slow cooker stoneware, use a vegetable nonstick spray. Or use cake pan grease, which is available in specialty cake-decorating or bulk-food stores.

1 cup	all-purpose flour	250 mL
2 tsp	baking powder	10 mL
3/4 cup	granulated sugar	175 mL
3 tbsp	cocoa	45 mL
1/2 cup	milk	125 mL
2 tbsp	butter, melted	25 mL
1 tsp	vanilla	5 mL
1/4 cup	chopped walnuts (optional)	50 mL
3/4 cup	packed brown sugar	175 mL
2 tbsp	cocoa	25 mL
2 cups	boiling water	500 mL
	Vanilla ice cream	

1. In a bowl combine flour, baking powder, sugar and cocoa; mix well.
2. In another bowl, combine milk, butter and vanilla. Stir into flour mixture and add walnuts. The batter will be very thick. Spread evenly in prepared slow cooker insert.
3. In a bowl combine brown sugar and cocoa. Add boiling water, mixing well. Pour over batter in slow cooker.
4. Cover and cook on **High** for 2 hours or until toothpick inserted in the center of the pudding comes out clean. Spoon into individual bowls and serve with scoops of vanilla ice cream.

Steamed Cranberry Pudding with Grand Marnier Sauce

Serves 6

6-CUP (1.5 L) PUDDING MOLD OR MIXING BOWL, LIGHTLY GREASED

1 cup	chopped cranberries, fresh or frozen (not thawed)	250 mL
3/4 cup	granulated sugar	175 mL
1/2 cup	butter, softened	125 mL
2	eggs	2
1 1/2 cups	all-purpose flour	375 mL
1 1/2 tsp	baking powder	7 mL
Pinch	salt	Pinch
2 tbsp	milk	25 mL
1 tbsp	grated orange zest	15 mL

GRAND MARNIER SAUCE

1/2 cup	packed brown sugar	125 mL
2 tbsp	cornstarch	25 mL
1/4 tsp	salt	1 mL
1 1/2 cups	water	375 mL
2 tbsp	butter	25 mL
3 tbsp	Grand Marnier *or* any orange liqueur *or* orange juice concentrate	45 mL

This cranberry-dotted pudding comes from Carol Ferguson and *Canadian Living* magazine. It's a pleasant alternative to traditional holiday plum pudding, although it can be enjoyed at any time of the year.

TIP

You will need to use a large (5- to 6 1/2-quart) slow cooker so your pudding mold will fit and can be easily removed. Be sure to use long oven mitts when lifting out the mold, so the steam doesn't burn your arms.

If you have an old-fashioned pudding bowl with a lid, it will be ideal for this recipe. But a 6-cup (1.5 L) heavy glass mixing bowl will work equally well.

1. In a bowl toss together cranberries and 1/4 cup (50 mL) of the sugar. Set aside.

2. In a bowl with an electric mixer, cream butter. Add remaining 1/2 cup (125 mL) sugar and beat until light and fluffy. Beat in eggs, one at a time.

3. In another bowl, stir together flour, baking powder and salt. Add to butter mixture, a little at a time, alternately with milk. (Mixture will be very thick.) Stir in orange zest. Spoon into prepared pudding mold or heavy bowl. Cover with lid or foil and secure with elastic band. Place in slow cooker and pour in enough boiling water to come 1 inch (2.5 cm) up sides of bowl.

4. Cover and cook on **High** for 4 1/2 to 5 hours or until toothpick inserted in center of pudding comes out clean. (Pudding will look slightly moist around the outside edges.) Remove from slow cooker and let stand for 10 minutes to cool. Turn out onto a serving plate.

5. Grand Marnier Sauce: In a saucepan over medium-high heat, combine brown sugar, cornstarch and salt. Stir in water and bring mixture to a boil. Reduce heat to medium and cook, whisking constantly, for 3 minutes or until thickened. Stir in butter and Grand Marnier, adding more liqueur if desired. Serve sauce spooned over pudding or in a sauce boat to pass at the table.

Very Adult Rice Pudding

Serves 4 to 6

1	can (13 oz [385 mL]) evaporated milk	1
2 tbsp	brown sugar	25 mL
3 tbsp	butter, melted	45 mL
1 tsp	vanilla	5 mL
1	egg, lightly beaten	1
1 tsp	lemon juice	5 mL
1/2 cup	dried cranberries or cherries	125 mL
2 cups	cooked rice	500 mL
1/4 tsp	cinnamon	1 mL
	Grand Marnier, Amaretto or dark rum	
	Whipped cream	

This is true comfort food – rich, satisfying and oh-so creamy.

TIP

If using rum, make sure it's the dark type. White rum will give this dish an unpleasantly metallic flavor.

MAKE AHEAD

This dish is best made the day before to give the flavors the opportunity to blend and develop.

1. In a bowl combine milk, sugar, butter, vanilla, egg, lemon juice and cranberries, mixing well.
2. Place rice in prepared slow cooker insert. Pour milk mixture over rice and sprinkle with cinnamon.
3. Cover and cook on **High** for 2 hours (do not cook for a longer time on **Low**) or until top is set and a toothpick inserted in the center of the pudding comes out clean. Spoon into serving bowls and drizzle with Grand Marnier and a dollop of whipped cream.

Index

Vegetable(s) (continued):
  -lentil soup, 49
  Moroccan hotpot, 86
  pastitsio, 80-81
  root,
    with balsamic vinegar, 157
    and sausage casserole, 129
  and turkey stew, 151
Vegetarian chili, 69, 70, 71

W

Walnuts, curried, 27
White pea beans:
  chicken and corn chili, 72
  molasses baked, 76
  turkey chili, 69
Wild rice:
  about, 161
  pecan mushroom, 161
Wine:
  choosing, 34
  mulled red, 34
Winterberry warmers, 35

Z

Zesty orange beef stew, 116